Fishing for Change
Tales From a Galloway
Guest House

KEN BARLOW

This paperback edition July 2021

Cover photo credits:
Main Picture © Peter Foster
Carp Picture (back cover) © Mark Stone

ISBN: 978-0-9562380-4-7

Dedicated to my wife Jackie, and my two daughters Adele and Emma who accompanied me throughout the journey.

And . . .

To my kid brother Robbie, sadly taken far too soon and without whose generosity this book would not have seen the light of day.

CONTENTS

AUTHOR'S NOTE

All details contained within these pages are either to the best of my recollection or as passed on to me by others. I apologise if I have unintentionally offended anyone, this was not my intent.

Where I felt it appropriate to do so I have made people anonymous or changed their names.

Thanks to everyone who contributed to this story, knowingly or otherwise!

INTRODUCTION

As Groundhog Days go, this one was right up there with the best. I was up to my oxsters in muddy water, surrounded by a forest of reeds and weeds, when a visiting angler suggested the blindingly bloody obvious. "Tha' needs a mini-digger for that lot," he proffered. "No, I hadn't thought of that," I muttered under my breath. "I have one back 'ome, didn't bring it on 'oliday like," he stated with no hint of intended humour.

My back ached and my feet were blistered, while my hands and arms throbbed in pain. Cold, muddy water cascaded over the top of my chest-waders, seeking places I didn't know I still had, causing sensations I hadn't felt since I was a little boy. (Well there was that one time . . . although perhaps that's a story better left for another day.)

Peering through stinging, sweat-blurred eyes, there, just visible midst a jungle of reed mace and lilies, was the uplifting sight of an old friend, and my target for today's labours.

Twenty years previously, I had sent my old wooden work boat to the great boat yard in the sky (or under the water in this case). Having served me well but like the rest of us, prone to the leaks and splintering of old age, I drove a stake through her heart and fixed her in the corner of a swim, creating a fish-friendly feature and a lasting and self-serving monument.

In the many years that had passed since I gave up the fishing rights to the loch concerned, Glendarroch Loch, the boat, along with most of the swims, had become choked up from neglect as mother nature re-established her domain. Now I had taken the fishing rights back I faced the daunting task of clearing the swims all over again to allow me to fish.

Slowly and painfully, hour after hour, clearing tons of weeds along the way, I edged gradually toward my long-lost boat. Midst curses and stumbles, and patiently ignoring irritating and unhelpful comments from onlookers, all of whom were experts at weed removal, I put a question to myself. *I first started out with this carry-on in 1991; just how the hell have I ended up doing it all over again?*

For those readers who believe 'fishing' to be about more than just catching fish, perhaps the answer to this rhetorical question will become evident as you read on . . .

1 THE ART OF DROWNING MAGGOTS

L ooking back, it is difficult to establish the point in my life at which fishing took such control. In 1958, as a young boy aged four, I recall being given the privilege of looking through my grandfather's tackle box. It lived in the garage, musty and unused. But the bright colours of the floats, the tiny hooks, the slender, reed rods and the various contraptions that I could only guess at the use of; all of these utterly intrigued me. (I still have one of his quill floats in my tackle box to this day.)

Aged eight and having never caught a fish with rod and line, I wrote a project for school that involved drawing all the UK species of freshwater fish. I revealed their common names and their Latin names, where they could be found, and how best to catch them. I even coloured in all the sketches. (I recall my pike looking like a barracuda.) It seemed to take me forever, and I enjoyed every moment of it. Why couldn't all education be so engaging? I earned rich praise from an astonished teacher; astonished because I had shown no such conscientious endeavour previously, (nor since). Perhaps it was the hard-wired 'hunter-gather' in me, showing himself at an early stage.

For most of the early years of my life I lived in Worsley, Salford. So did my maternal grandparents, who lived very close to the

Bridgewater Canal. The Bridgewater Canal, for those who have never seen it, is a peculiar orange/copper colour. I recall being amazed that anything could live in such water, let alone the large numbers of roach that positively thrived in its murky shallows.

The colour of this particular waterway is apparently due to copper, released by the coal workings at the canal's source. Accessing and then transporting this coal was what led to the canal being built in the 18th century by James Brindley, thus laying claim to be the first canal in the UK. While the mines ceased working many years ago, the copper still leeches into the water to the present day. My grandfather was awarded the OBE for his services to The Manchester Ship Canal as Chief Engineer, so there was perhaps some symmetry in my canal intrigue.

My mother could recall being taken fishing by my granddad when she was young. Much to my rather snooty grandma's disgust, she was allowed to actually handle the maggots, or 'gentles' as they were called then. ("don't you dare tell the neighbours,") but sadly, Granddad died before I was deemed old enough to safely accompany him on any fishing trips. I do however remember walks with him along the canal footpath as he chatted to hoary old anglers wearing rolled down wellies and duffle-coats, boiler-suits or donkey jackets. Such walks would invariably include inspections of the contents of many keep-nets along the way.

Perhaps it was this early inoculation that laid the foundations for my fishing passion. If so, it was a short 'jab', because I only ever recall actually fishing the Bridgewater Canal once or twice, and that was with my 'Uncle' Ernie Walsh a few years later. He spent most of the first session walking a long way to cross the nearest bridge in order to retrieve my terminal tackle from the opposite bank and then traipse back again. Ten minutes later he would have to start the whole process again. (Eventually we moved nearer the bridge.) His patience was unbounded, and I owe him a great debt of gratitude, although there have been times in my angling career when I wished he had just given up and dragged me home, never to fish again. It would have saved a whole lot of misery! Then again, I would have missed out on the great pleasure and camaraderie that a lifetime of angling has also given me.

One pivotal moment in my early fishing life arrived when I learned to swim. All my lessons in the local baths at Walkden had paid off, and I was allowed to go fishing alone. Although accompanied fishing was the preferred parental option, I could usually arrange matters to ensure that I was alone. I was a shy boy by nature – I still am, though I hide it well – and fishing appealed to me as a pastime to be enjoyed in one's own company. By and large, I still hold this to be true. The parental 'freedom to fish' rule opened up visits to various ponds near our home, where numerous sticklebacks and the odd hungry perch could be caught, using the clichéd 'bamboo cane and a bent pin'. I was 11 years old before I was given my own second-hand rod and reel, a four-foot glass fibre affair with a thumb grip, courtesy of Uncle Ernie. My catches improved not one jot.

At the age of 11, in 1965, my family moved from the idyllic surroundings of Worsley to the rather less aesthetically pleasing countenance of Wigan. Fishing, football and trainspotting continued to be my obsessions, as I adapted to new schools, new friends and a bewildering dialect. For example, "narladwestufromthee?", uttered as one long word, which translated means "Now young man, where are you from?"

I experimented in all the usual boyhood hobbies of the time, but continued to seek out opportunities for fishing. I became a frequent visitor to Haigh Canal, the Leeds-Liverpool Canal and various nearby pits and mill dams. My parents would pay for a rod licence for me, but day tickets were another matter, so I soon learnt to recognise the approaching sound of the bailiff's Honda 50. I could hide my bike, rod, tackle-box and self in a nearby hedge in two minutes flat. I suspect that often the bailiff knew exactly where I was, but turned a blind eye on the basis that it was better I was fishing than causing trouble on the streets of Wigan, as many of my peers were at that time.

I wish I could say that I honed my craft to an art form on the difficult waters around Wigan, but truth be told I usually struggled, and often caught nothing at all. I was too shy to ask the older anglers I came across for advice, and anyway, their gruff, monosyllabic and usually vulgar answers on the rare occasions when I did approach them for help, taught me not to ask too often.

Around this time, in the mid-1960's, unemployment in Wigan was high, the pits and mills were closed, and many engineering and manufacturing businesses were in decline. Frequently I would see anglers, usually older men, take fish home to supplement what was often a meagre family diet. These fish were rarely dispatched humanely, but rather were left flapping about in mortal agony within the depths of a shopping bag brought for the purpose. Any attempt to question the morality of this practice with these tough old anglers would lead to a clip around the ear and a clear invitation to leave the vicinity forthwith, or words to that effect. I did note that they rarely took fish when committee members were present. I always felt so sorry for the fish; I vowed never to do the same, and I never have. I suppose anglers of my generation were amongst the first to recognise the value of humane angling and good fish care, while thankfully never being so poor as to need to steal fish for the table in the first place.

Whatever their morals, these old anglers were highly skilled at catching fish and I learned a lot just by watching them. I paid attention to their shot patterns, techniques like 'laying-on' and 'the lift method', their levels of concentration, the quality of bait, and even the times they actually started fishing. These things and many more gradually seeped into my ever growing angling data-base.

My dad did not fish. As a father of five children he rarely had time for any hobbies other than DIY and car maintenance. He did give me a tip once, however. As I set off on my bike to fish Haigh Canal in the pouring rain, he suggested I stay under a bridge; I could keep dry and avoid the worst of the weather, while the fish would congregate there, he reasoned. As young teenagers are wont to do, I paid little heed to the actual content of my dad's words, but did as I was told with blind obedience. It was only after an hour or so of blanking under a bridge that I pondered on what he'd said, and felt such a fool. I rarely listened to him anyway at that age, and that trick hadn't helped. I moved from under the bridge, becoming sodden wet as I fished on relentlessly, and guess what?

I still caught nothing.

As the years passed, so my interests gradually turned elsewhere. I became obsessed with Wigan Athletic Football Club, then a lowly non-league team. (See 'Mild & Bitter Were the Days' for stories of my life as a 16 year-old daft lad in Wigan, 1970.)

Football, beer and girls, in that order, took preference over drowning maggots in t'cut, (the canal). My fishing days gradually dwindled to virtually nil.

However, by 1978, and not long married, my darling wife, presumably keen to get me out from under her feet, bought me a basic 'starter kit' for anglers, and my latent love of fishing was rekindled. My family had previously moved up to Tyneside, but by this point in my independent life I was living in Warrington, Cheshire, and I enjoyed exploring local ponds and the nearby Cheshire meres. I occasionally returned to my old haunts in the Wigan area, largely for nostalgic purposes I suspect, because I fared no better in terms of angling results.

1981 saw me return to the North East of England, where Marden Quarry in Whitley Bay was a favourite spot for me to catch carp. The local angling club, 'Big Waters A.C.' had very obligingly just stocked the water heavily, as if preparing for my arrival on the scene.

Coarse fishing on Tyneside was very much in the shadow of game and sea fishing, but we band of brothers found plenty of action exploring rivers and lakes from Berwick in the north to Ripon in

Yorkshire to the south.

Trips to Ireland and friendly matches with Wansbeck and District Angling Club cemented my love for angling; it was just a short step to make it my life.

2 TOO MUCH THINKING IS A DANGEROUS THING . . .

The Metro train eased its way into the next suburban station having seemingly only pulled away from the previous stop a matter of minutes before. The windows were steamed up, and wiping them clear proved to be a futile gesture. What little could be seen consisted of the back gardens and allotments of North Tyneside, with water barrels humorously marked '*IPA*,' '*Brown*' and '*Bitter*,' before giving way to murky industrial estates as the train interminably inched its way toward Newcastle-upon-Tyne city centre.

The same faces would board and alight at the same stations every day. Pretty faces, grizzled faces and, like mine, bored faces, all undertaking the same journey as yesterday, and the day before that, and the week/month before that. Indeed, the same journey for the previous however many years in some cases. Many of my fellow travellers would be engrossed in books or newspapers; or at least they appeared to be. For such a friendly race, the Geordie Nation had unusually acquired the social nuance common to London Tube travellers of refusing to speak to one another on the train. In shops, pubs, queues or anywhere else, silence was anathema to the average Geordie, but on the Metro, it was a social pre-requisite.

I would sit and observe people – a lifetime hobby of mine. I would attribute occupations, backgrounds, and even names to total strangers. The secretary, the student, the school teacher, the redundant ship-worker re-training in I.T. . . . . all would be pigeon-holed as I passed the time of day. It was uncanny how often I would subsequently be proven correct, were I to chance across these people in their day to day settings, as would occasionally happen.

My internal dialogue would run something like this: *What about that chap in his sixties sat opposite me? He has receding, grey hair, pallid features, is probably still in the same job he's held for the past 50 years and possibly dreading retirement, old age, frailty and eventual death. Will that be me in 30 years' time? Am I looking in a time warp mirror?*

As the journey progressed I would survey the day ahead, dreading anticipated problems. I would rehearse the possible tangents my chaotic day might fly off at, shudder under the responsibilities I felt keenly, yet simultaneously relish the challenges I might face with confidence.

Thinking too profoundly for too long is never a good thing, at least it isn't for me. I would inevitably arrive at the conclusion that there must surely be more to life than this.

'Sir' Bob Geldof allegedly once claimed that he went into pop music to "get rich, get famous and to get laid." I couldn't relate to these aspirations, much as I might have wished to do so, but like Sir Bob I didn't like Mondays, while the title of his autobiography, *Is That It?* struck a disconcerting chord with me.

Changes

In the mid-1980s, after many years in mental health nursing practise, I had moved into nurse education, working as a 'Nurse Tutor'. This involved me helping experienced mental health nurses to adapt their skills, knowledge and attitudes from institutional based care to community care. When political policies saw this particular specialised educational course close, I found myself being moved to a teaching post that involved nurturing two groups of 15 people, often young, through a three-year training programme to become Registered Mental

Health Nurses.

I well recall one morning when one of the students stated, "You do realise that we can never put into practice what you teach us, don't you?" There followed a chorus of agreement from the remainder of the group. Over the next half-hour a discussion ensued, based around the need to identify where changes in nursing practise were needed, and how their educational programme aimed to empower them to lead such changes. "What you teach us is all fine and dandy," they insisted, "but we leave college all fired up, then hit the real world out there both on the wards and in the community, where it all turns 'tits up'."

The group's concerns, that they felt unable to turn the college-based theory into skill-based practice, were disconcerting, and gave me much food for thought. Was I really wasting my time and at the same time colluding with an educational and political system that deceived the students and their patients? I concluded that in the climate of the time, I probably was. Furthermore, I was deceiving myself into believing my career was a worthy one.

That evening, I went fishing.

"And just what is so terribly wrong with that?", squealed an indignant ward Sister when I challenged her policy of re-using dry incontinence pads. I stared at her with utter disbelief written across my face and replied, "Do you honestly believe it to be good nursing practice to have your elderly patients wear a pad all night, then take it off in the morning and re-use it again later that night? Would you do that to yourself, or to your own mother?"

She retorted, "I believe it is good practice to bring my monthly budgets in under target, so my manager can maximise the limited resources allocated to us."

The young, inexperienced Sister, promoted above her abilities in my humble opinion, gradually turned red in the face. She was clearly both embarrassed, and at the same time angry, that some jumped up half-wit, as she clearly perceived me to be, should descend upon her little empire from the ivory towers of academia to challenge what had become accepted and acceptable practice. What dispirited me utterly wasn't her response; I was used to such management rhetoric. This was after all, a time when the NHS had been reduced to an artificially contrived 'competitive market'. Rather it was the fact that here was a ward Sister who clearly felt so omnipotent in a financially-judged milieu that she believed no one had the right to challenge her decision making on the grounds of acceptable, basic nursing care. Had it really come to this I wondered?

That evening, I went fishing.

"Project 2000 will change UK Nurse Education for better, for ever," thundered the Director of Nursing. "We, as educationalists must be prepared to value and embrace this change. It is incumbent upon us to drive the changes needed to bring nurse education into a new dawn." It was hard to hide my contempt for such over-hyped cant and hypocrisy. My colleagues and I knew that it was merely hyperbole, aimed at justifying the move away from NHS-controlled nurse education to the newly created 'stand-alone' city universities, (polytechnics by their previous name).

We also knew that as individual tutors and as teaching institutions, we were not well prepared for the changes that were about to overwhelm us. Neither philosophically, educationally, nor by way of learning environments. The first intake of 'P2000' students proved my concerns to be utterly justified.

My first session saw a group of 50 students crammed into a classroom designed for 20. Many had to sit on the floor. It was unbearably hot, stuffy and noisy, as the students found it hard to concentrate and reverted to chatting amongst themselves.

The next teaching session I was allocated to take was located in a huge lecture hall at the nearby university. Here I had 120 students to whom I was expected to impart one of the most crucial aspects of the entire curriculum; *The Use of Self and Self-Awareness in Mental Health Nursing.'*

Previously this topic would involve a two-hour session to a dozen students, and would be based upon small group work, experiential teaching practice and much discussion around self-disclosure, building rapport and establishing trust, and would 'spiral' throughout the curriculum. The P2000 students were given an allocated straight lecture of 30 minutes' duration before all shuffling off, seemingly bored rigid, to their next session.

My Senior Lecturer congratulated me on my ability to change the content and format of the session in line with new expectations.

I pondered, on my way home to my wife and two young daughters. *Has it really come to this? Is this really what I will be expected to do for the next 30 years?* I understood that some of the issues were just teething problems, but I also realised that henceforth, nurse education would be judged on the number of recruits to any given course; bums on seats and graduation numbers, in other words, quantity not quality. The *quality* of the learning experience would, in my opinion, inevitably come a sorry second.

That night, I didn't go fishing.

Rather, I went to the RAFA Club in Whitley Bay where, as on most Friday nights, I played darts badly for the club team. I would drink nine pints of best bitter then buy cod and chips on the way home enjoying each indulgence to the same degree. My work colleague and friend Chris and I would put the world to rights as we meandered home. Change in my life just had to happen.

And so life continued, until one day . . .

Our family holidays were spent in a caravan in Kirkcudbright, Dumfries and Galloway, Scotland. My wife and I enjoyed it, the kids loved it. This was a real change of pace and scenery. I would endeavour to have accrued enough brownie points in the marital bank to earn a 'pass' for couple of days fishing. For some years nearby Loch Ken was the likeliest venue; it was a radical change from the canals, ponds and rivers I was used to, more of which much later.

One of the benefits of fishing is the time it allows for free, conscious thought. On one level I would concentrate on the job in hand, catching fish. On another, my reveries would wander back to my dissatisfaction with my life.

It is so easy to fantasize when in holiday mode. *Wouldn't it be great to live and work here? I could get a job, any job. We would live in a cottage in a small village, my flaxen-haired kids would frolic in golden fields of corn and all would be well with my world.* At this point, reality would pierce my subconscious thoughts with the realisation that my maggot box had spilt and the contents escaped. Common sense would interject like the impact of a six-ounce lead cast from a beach-caster. I had a career, a mortgage, a wife and kids. So it's back to the grindstone for you, my boy. Oh, and by the way, just be grateful for your lot.

At some point in the mid-1980s I had discovered a wonderful private loch stuffed full of tench, my favourite quarry. Craichlaw Loch was picturesque, secluded and rarely fished. Situated in the private grounds of a country house, it was surrounded by rhododendrons. With extensive lily pads, an island and even a boat house, it was my idea of angling heaven.

As anyone who has fished with me will tell you, I am not the best angler in the world, and any place that saw me catch up to a dozen tench at a session was good enough for me. The tench fought like barbel, and if they weren't feeding, the roach and rudd would usually oblige. There were a few large carp and even some bream present, but I had too much fun with the tench to target other species.

Day tickets for Craichlaw were bought from a guest house in the nearby market town of Newton Stewart – 'The Palakona Guest House' – and over the years I became a frequent visitor to the loch. So frequent that my mother and step-father, who had moved up to the area some years previously, bought me a season ticket as a birthday present. How do mothers intuitively know just what is 'right' for you?

I would travel from the caravan in Kirkcudbright for dawn sessions. Unfortunately this meant leaving in the early hours. Stumbling around in a darkened caravan usually meant awakening the whole family; this was not considered good form. It also meant I would return, midge-bitten, bleary-eyed and sleepy for what little of the day remained. But it was my holiday too, I would tell myself, to rationalise my actions.

On my way back from such fishing trips I would invariably call in at the Palakona and inform the proprietor, a Yorkshireman whom I shall call Leon, of my success or otherwise. We became quite friendly, and it was on one such occasion that he casually informed me that he may not be there the next time I called in because he was putting the guest house on the market. And yes, for a brief nanosecond, the thought of buying it flashed through my mind. The idea never took root and was dismissed immediately as just another absurd fantasy; I didn't even mention it to my wife, Jackie.

'Knock Hard, Life is Deaf'

A year later, on an Easter break in the spring of 1990, I was negotiating a sudden hail storm as we drove past Loch Ken when Jackie asked me if I'd be going fishing. "Well not in this bloody weather!", I retorted in a typically grumpy manner, before going on to mention that there was some doubt if I could fish Craichlaw Loch anyway as Leon had put the guest house on the market. "You never told me that," she replied. "Is that not something you think we could have a crack at?"

I don't think I've ever loved my wife more than at that precise moment.

To be fair, Jackie had also been yearning for something different in her life. She, too, worked as a mental health nurse, and she, too, felt dissatisfied with her lot. She had often mentioned her dream of opening a tea room or café. The more challenging idea of running a guest house and fishery appeared not to worry her one bit.

A brief phone call later that day established that the Palakona was still on the market, and this led to some serious thinking on our part.

We had to work through the wishful thinking and consider the harsh reality. This was a major decision in our lives, and most importantly, in that of our two children. We had careers to throw away, a four-bedroom semi in a seaside resort to give up. It would mean the children losing friends and moving schools, then settling into a different country. (And if any reader believes that Scotland is not a different country they should try telling that to the Scots and then stand well back!)

On our return home we canvassed the opinions of family, friends, and work colleagues. We spoke to bank managers, estate agents and solicitors. We listened to every point of view and despite stark warnings from many, given that the UK was heading for a recession, we decided to go ahead and turn our world upside down.

One of the telling factors for me was that if I proceeded I could answer the question, *Is that it?* with the firm answer *No, there's more to come!*

In addition, my experiences as a nurse of the distressing effects of ill health has meant that I always see life as an experience to enjoy, rather than a series of travails to be overcome before the grim reaper comes a-calling. If you have to knock hard to get life to listen then so be it, I was knocking.

So it was that after assuring the bank manager that my nursing qualifications should offer reasonable prospects for employment should things not work out, and having bribed the kids with prospects of owning ponies (regrettably they never did), we began the tricky process of negotiating the purchase of The Palakona Guest House.

This took many months, and involved various twists and turns. The previously friendly vendor Leon turned somewhat less friendly, as his economy with the truth became increasingly apparent. He claimed to have leases on various local waters; we asked for details of these, only to discover that he had a lease agreement with just one riparian owner and even this was non-transferable.

We asked for a precise value of the fish stocks in the only loch that he still had a formal lease for, and for him to explain how he arrived at the figures he came up with to justify these being a saleable asset in the asking price. He was unable to provide this. Understandably so, I suppose; it's not easy to do a stock-check when your stock items live nine feet down in six acres of water – just as you'd start to count the little beggars they'd swim away and you'd have to start again! Nevertheless, he'd placed the considerable sum of approximately £30,000 on stock, so you can see why we felt we had to ask.

We asked for a current, valid fire certificate. Again, Leon was unable to provide one. Despite numerous protestations that he couldn't quite put his hands on it, it transpired that the certificate in question had expired a few years previously, and he had declined to renew it. He claimed he had simply forgotten this fact.

The dishwasher was waiting for new parts, the grill likewise, while the microwave had mysteriously vanished. Legs were missing off some of the beds (propped up by books) and guests even had to put 10p pieces in meters to activate the electric heaters in the bedrooms!

Despite assurances that the bookings diary was full, it turned out that The Palakona Guest House had only one advance booking in place, (and no deposit for that).

I could continue with many other examples of the difficulties we faced in the negotiations, but I hope I've given an idea of just how painstaking our investigations had to be. All of this led to delays in confirming the mortgage, or business loan as it turned out to be. Our bank manager followed the various comings and goings with great interest but to be fair, with equal commitment to our ultimate aims.

We were fortunate to have engaged a local solicitor who knew the previous owner and understood the situation well. His due diligence saved us from financial disaster. This was ironic, really, because just a short time later the very same solicitor was found to have been embezzling client's monies and was eventually sent to prison and debarred from practice as a solicitor 'sine die'. It seemed it was pure, good fortune on our part that he chose not to use our monies for his own ends, though many local people suffered badly, remaining out of pocket to this day.

Eventually, many months later than we'd planned, our house was sold and the guest house deal concluded. A reduced price was agreed, with an added financial retention arranged to cover any and all costs appertaining to any works that needed to be completed in order for the property to be issued with a valid fire certificate. The missives were agreed and the forms signed. Even this simple process meant a trip from Tyneside to Dumfries, to be advised by a Scottish solicitor to ensure we understood the differences in mortgage arrangements as enshrined within Scottish, as opposed to English, law. This was a pointless exercise, as the entire interface was conducted using legal and financial jargon and we emerged no wiser, having just nodded at appropriate moments then signed the forms as they were presented to us. *What a carry on*, I mused, *all this, just to change your life completely.*

I handed in my notice at work and our neighbours organised a farewell party, as did my students and colleagues. We hired a van and with the help of my family, we packed up most of our worldly possessions. It was a small van, and despite cramming and squeezing we were forced to leave some things behind, the lawn mower being one such item. The car was also stuffed full of all those essentials that you just can't leave behind, like the kids, the wife and the cat. This was a one-way trip.

3 WHAT HAVE WE DONE?

It was the summer of 1991.

We moved in at the end of May, but the exuberance and excitement of the move was short-lived. The entire guest house needed cleaning from top to bottom. Cooking oil and fats had been left encrusted on kitchen utensils and appliances over many years; these were prised off with an initial enthusiasm and vigour that soon wore off. The bedroom carpets were lifted, and the rooms cleaned from the floorboards up. Fortunately, friends and family all pitched in to help with these and many other tasks; we were very grateful at the time, and remain so to this day.

The Palakona Guest House was a mid-terraced building fronting onto the main road of Newton Stewart, with views to the rear across the River Cree and out onto Cairnsmore, one of the many scenic Galloway Hills. An arched alleyway gave shared access to the rear car-park, buildings and a lengthy garden. Named after a Spanish cane used in rod-building, the Palakona was reputedly an old coaching inn, and the archway had two large granite blocks on either side at the base of the entrance purportedly positioned to govern the width of the coaches that were permitted access.

The property consisted of eight bedrooms, a large lounge/dining room, a smaller lounge, a kitchen and various outbuildings. The building also had many idiosyncrasies that only revealed themselves to us gradually, and by trial and error. I endeavoured to get other people to undertake the 'trial and error' bit; it seemed safer that way.

My good friend of many years Glyn was one of these volunteers, and a DIY enthusiast to boot. He came to stay for a week to help with some of the renovations. It was immensely kind of him. His kindness was particularly apparent when it came to testing bare electrical cables with his screwdriver. It transpired that turning off the building's entire electrical supply at the mains was an inadequate precaution to take in this ancient house because as he did so there was a flash and a loud bang. Poor Glyn was blown over to the other side of the room where he slumped to the floor, dazed and shaken, muttering, "That just can't happen; it's simply not scientifically possible."

When I stopped laughing, I asked him if the experience had been a bit of a shock. For some reason, he didn't find my comment funny. "Oh, come on mate, I'm only trying to make light of it . . . " I added. That didn't raise so much as a smile, either.

There were some beneficial side effects for Glyn, though. The incident certainly cleared any potential constipation problems he might have had, or latent depression, while at the same time it provided him with a frizzy and fashionable perm to bolster his rapidly thinning hair. Sadly, neither the electro-perm nor the hair itself lasted much longer.

Power Rangers?

Some detective work, coupled with testing by our electrician, eventually solved the mystery of the rogue, live circuit. Apparently, a few years earlier the previous owner had also purchased the house next door. He converted both houses into one much larger guest house, and centralised the electrical supplies accordingly. However, this state of affairs did not last long, and a hasty sale of the next door property had taken place. So hasty, in fact, that somehow part of the power supply wasn't reinstated properly when the house was sold. Not only were certain parts of the electrical system still being sourced from next door, but the occupants there had been paying for it, too! Our electrician swiftly rectified the matter, but this wasn't the end of the matter.

The doorbell rang one morning, and I opened it to be confronted by two men in high-viz jackets flourishing ID cards in an authoritative, indeed confrontational manner.

They were from the electricity supply company. I let them in, thinking they'd come to read the meter. Well they had . . . sort of.

"My name is **** and this is my colleague, ****," one of the men began. "Are you the proprietor? We are here to serve a summons upon you for tampering with the electricity supply to the address of ***** in contravention of the**** Act of 19**. . . " On and on they went, reeling off what was clearly a well-rehearsed mantra that they probably repeated in their sleep. They left no room for interruption or explanation on my part.

To cut a long story short, I became annoyed when one of them tried to physically force a piece of paper – some kind of legal document – upon my person, while at the same time his colleague proceeded to break open the meter cupboard.

They must have missed the training sessions when listening skills were being taught.

Eventually, and only then with a raised voice and angry hand movements, was I able to intervene, explaining that while I was indeed the *current* proprietor (no pun intended), I hadn't been so at the time and date they referred to when the offence had apparently taken place.

"Oh, so you are not a Mr ********?"

At last the penny dropped, and they ceased their pseudo-police officer, authoritarian approach and started to speak to me in a civil manner.

It transpired that the issue was not only that the power supply had been misappropriated. The electricity company official asked me to look very closely at the meter, and in particular the rotating disc. Sure enough, tucked away at the rear of the unit, a minute hole had been drilled through the casing, into which had been inserted what looked like micro-thin fuse-wire. Apparently, this wire slowed down the rotation of the disc, thus reducing the rate of recorded power being used. I didn't quite understand the mechanics of it, but I knew nothing about it. I did wonder who had tipped them off to look for it in the first place, though. The bailiffs apologised, and were soon on their way. I never heard any more about the matter, but the meter was replaced by a modern digital one within a few short days.

On Meeting One of the Locals

Newton Stewart is a (sometimes) bustling market town, nestled in the Scottish Galloway Hills. It has a population of about four thousand folk, most of whom are friendly and welcoming. In a small community certain characters stand out; I shall introduce some of them as the story unfolds.

As a newcomer, I explored the immediate vicinity to our new home with my dog, Clare. On one such occasion during that first week or so I went for a dog walk, leaving Glyn to his DIY. I came across a group of local youngsters singing loudly while taunting very large local woman.

"*Here she comes, Highland Annie, two big tits and a hairy fanny . . .*" they sang, repeatedly, while dancing around her from what they thought was a safe distance.

"Come here ya wee baastaads, I ken yoor mutha, I'll be at your hoose, see if I don't!" she responded vehemently, with slurred speech, as they skipped away from her hefty arms and well-aimed empty cans of lager. *God bless the lass*, I thought. She was aged about 20, she was large, and the 'foul language fairy' had clearly whispered in her ear on many an occasion. I wondered about intervening but . . . well, basically I was just too cowardly to do so and continued on my dog walk.

That night Glyn and I felt we deserved a few drinks and visited one of the many local pubs, The Black Horse. Apart from washing out the dust and grime from a hard day's work, I rationalised that it was important to remain hydrated; electrolyte balance had to be maintained, after all.

We ordered a pint, and Glyn put his money down on the pool table for a game. The next thing I knew, from the ladies emerged the same 'Highland Annie' from my previous encounter earlier in the day! Looking larger than life, she had clearly been taking a drink well before Glyn and I arrived. A few minutes later, she shouted across the room in our direction.

"Yee playing fucking pool or what?"

Glyn looked at me with terror in his eyes. "You play her, you're a local now – please, please?" he implored. But this was too good an opportunity to miss, so I politely declined his request, pointing out that he had put the 50p on the pool table in the first place. "Call yourself a mate," he muttered, "I'll make this quick and hope to escape with my bollocks intact."

Annie was a far better player than Glyn, but despite the veil of alcohol she was peering through she could see Glyn was barely trying. Eventually, she exploded. "Wot the fuck's up wi ye? Yur no even fuckin' tryin, ya wee English baastaad, ye."

She pinned him to the wall with her pool cue, and basically accused him of taking the piss. Her pride was hurt, and she wasn't for having it. Glyn could taste the vodka and coke as spittle spattered across his face. "Err, no, no not all . . . I'm just crap at pool," he explained.

I sat in the corner, smirking. (you were allowed to smirk in pubs in 1991, before the *No Smirking'* ban.) Glyn did try slightly harder for the next few shots and managed to massage Annie's ego enough to avoid any more outbursts, but she won the game easily and didn't offer to shake hands at the end. Meanwhile I had timed the emptying of my pint to coincide with the end of the game, and slid out of the pub barely concealing my mirth.

The Neglected Baby

All this domestic DIY stuff was fine and dandy for some, but after a few days of being trapped in the guest house I was desperate to start work on our other source of income, and my 'baby', the fishery. This particular baby presented as a serious case of 'failure to thrive'; a case conference and action plan were sorely needed.

On purchasing the business I'd discovered that the only actual water I had formal fishing rights to was Craichlaw Loch, some seven miles from the guest house, and even these rights had only been granted as a result of negotiation with the owner, Mr Andrew Gladstone, during the previous few months. Andrew was, and remains, a gentleman in such matters.

Craichlaw Loch was originally created as a curling loch – a loch created to facilitate that quintessentially Scottish winter sport of curling – and is understood to be the second oldest of its kind in Scotland. It's a beautiful six and a quarter acre body of water, located in the grounds of Craichlaw House. There is evidence of a medieval keep on the site, and a Tower House was built in 1664. The current house was rebuilt in1864, which I'm pretty sure is roughly the same era as my fishing tackle.

Craichlaw Loch.

Surrounded by rhododendrons and edged with colourful lilies, the loch also hosts an island, two bridges and even a stone-built boat house. It was as if an English home-counties estate lake of 'Capability Brown'-style design had been magically transported a few hundred miles across the border to Scotland. Wildlife thrived within the proximity of the loch, with deer, red squirrels, foxes, and badgers frequently seen by anglers. On the down side, so were midges, cormorants, otters and herons, with the occasional mink paying us a visit.

Access to the loch was granted via the main drive up to the house and this shared access was to prove problematic from the start, as certain coarse anglers ignored the rules, as they are prone to do. They parked their cars wherever took their fancy, bivvied up, enjoyed barbeques, and fished just about wherever they wanted to. For too many years visiting anglers had enjoyed freedom to roam with very limited bailiffing. Many had enjoyed private arrangements with the previous fishing rights owner, and were reluctant to relinquish these. Exhortations along the lines of "But the previous chap always let me park on the drive/pay at the end of the week/let my dog run free/set up six rods/have a barbeque . . ." etcetera, were commonplace. I referred the culprits to said previous owner, if they could find him, and gave them copies of the new rules to read as they went on their way.

Controlling anglers was just one of the issues I had to face. As a fishery, the loch was in a mess, as a diary entry from June of that year suggests:

> The loch is in a real state. Boat sunk, pallets rotten, weeds overgrown and signs unreadable.
> Action plan:
> 1) Assess needs,
> 2) Decide priorities,
> 3) Consider costs,
> 4) Assemble materials.
> 5) ACTION!
> Rotten pallets removed, bridge temporarily repaired, Swims cut where possible, some are lost for ever, I fear.
> Tench feeding freely. Roach and Rudd to 2lb being caught.

In truth, one of the lessons I was to learn over subsequent years was that in rural matters Mother Nature is in charge, and as such she invariably dictates your priorities. Many of the swims were unfishable due to either overgrown bank-side vegetation, or aquatic weed growth. Water fowl walked across large parts of the loch, while the fish battled for open water in which to swim. In anticipation of the handover of control, the previous owner had failed to undertake any maintenance for a couple of years; now it was all down to me. Yippee! I couldn't wait, and I had come prepared. Weed clearance and bank-side access were clearly the priorities.

One advantage of having moved from Tyneside was that I didn't lack in support from the engineering sector. Family and friends had kindly provided me with all kinds of weed-cutting implements, from basic T-bars to a vicious-looking triangular band-saw contraption. The latter was particularly dangerous, with a deadly attraction to waders, Wellington boots and human flesh.

A polyethylene pipe ran through the centre of the loch, tethered to the bottom. This provided mains water to the 'big house', and was frequently at risk of being severed – I had to be very careful where I used these sharp-teethed, saw-blade cutters. Unfortunately they were less than effective in cutting their intended targets of weeds and lilies, requiring a sawing action to work properly. After adding numerous patches on my waders and plasters to various parts of my anatomy, details of which we need not go into here, I consigned the saw-blade cutters to the work shed. To this day they lie in the dark, still shuffling and growling in anticipation at the first sniff of any potential passing victim.

The predatory weed-cutters with their latest 'kill'.

Long Live The Rope

There were times throughout this early honeymoon period of our lifestyle transformation when reality would bite as hard and as frequently as the local midges. On one such occasion, I nearly died.

Craichlaw Loch is shallow, and silted up for the most part. This is an ideal environment for the ever-invasive water lilies, and removing them was a real problem. Having discarded the vicious band-saw cutters, I relied on the basic but effective T-bar, which works by dragging the rope back at a certain pace and angle that allows the cutting edge of the T-bar to sheer through the lily stems. It was simple and repetitive, but bloody hard work! Frequent cutting in this manner kept the swims clear of lilies in the short term, but of course, all I was actually doing was pruning them, and at the height of the growing season fresh new shoots would invade the swim within a few weeks. I soon learnt that just as in a domestic garden, if you don't remove the roots, the weeds will remain and flourish.

I also gradually learnt that there is a technique that removes lily roots almost entirely. I have honed this technique into an art form over the years (hundreds attend my workshop demonstrations), and found it to be by far the most effective way of permanently removing lilies from a swim, with the exception perhaps of a mechanical digger. I'll explain more about this later, but in those early days of May 1991 my enthusiasm outweighed sophistication, and it was this that so very nearly led to my early demise.

The day in question was mild and sunny, and the loch was deserted. I wore my chest waders and set about cutting a heavily weed-infested swim with great gusto, soon warming to the task. Hurling the T-bar ahead of me and watching with great satisfaction as it cut the lilies on its return, I soon had a large pile of lily leaves stems and roots (or *rhizomes*, to be accurate) behind me. It was hot and sweaty work, with rubber gloves essential. Said gloves and sweat in the eyes sometimes affected the accuracy of my throwing, and on one such occasion the T-bar landed in a particularly tangled area of the swim, where it became snagged on what proved to be a sodden, underwater log. Try as I might, it would not move. There was only one thing for it; I'd have to wade my way out into the shallow muddy water and retrieve the T-bar manually.

All went well, initially. I used the tension on the snagged rope to give me some purchase and as the swim was particularly shallow for the first ten yards or so, I was able to make steady progress, slowly wading out to the target.

Unbeknown to me, however, the swim suddenly shelved off, from three feet of water to five feet plus another two feet of silt, and all within a matter of one or two paces. Cold, muddy water poured over the top of my waders, filling them rapidly. At exactly this moment the

T-bar decided to come free from the snag, thus releasing the tension on the rope. I stumbled forward into deeper, muddier water, at which point I panicked slightly. I couldn't get any purchase underfoot; attempts to gain a footing were met with just silt while muddy water began to pour into my mouth and up my nose. I panicked again, more than just a little this time.

I remember thinking just how ridiculous this was; surely I wasn't going to drown in a shallow estate lake with only sniggering, vengeful tench for company? But it was all becoming very serious. As I thrashed around, desperately reaching out for anything at all to hold on to, my fingers became entangled in the rope. I was disoriented by now, and had unknowingly turned around to face the bank. As I instinctively pulled on the rope in desperation it suddenly tightened.

Of course! I had tied the rope to the base of a tree, to prevent it snaking out into the water if I was overly enthusiastic in my throwing action. Now that same precaution had saved me. I was able to pull myself along to safety, slowly but surely, using the rope for leverage. With chest waders full to brimming, I floundered my way to dry land, easing myself back over the shelf and crawling up the bank looking like the monster from a thousand fathoms. My face was covered in mud and slime while my hair was festooned with weeds, blood-worm, midges and various sub-aquatic life forms.

Minutes later I sat on the pile of previously excavated lilies, smoking a damp fag to help me expectorate the fetid gunge in my lungs and calm me down while trying to dry myself off. Recovering my poise, I recall thinking out loud, " . . . and just think, Kenny lad, you could be in a nice, dry lecture theatre right now!" Even at that soggy and sobering moment I wouldn't have changed places with my previous self for anything.

Furthermore, I'd recovered my precious T-bar.

I conveniently forgot to mention this incident to my wife for a few years, but I did vow that never again would I wade into unchartered waters alone. Even when I found I had no choice but to go solo, I always ensured I had a safety rope secured to a nearby tree. Well, nearly always.

Meanwhile . . .

The summer of 1991 proved to be a frantic and challenging one for all of us. My two daughters had quickly adapted to new schools and made new friends. My wife and I had to learn how to be hospitable guest house proprietors. Over the subsequent years Jackie managed this better than I. (A guest asked me once if my middle name was 'Basil'.) But in the very early stages of my new life, I was polite, diplomatic and tolerant. ("Yes madam, I do apologise; it *is* difficult to get the ITV Norwich news programme on the television, isn't it? Do you think it is possibly because we are in Scotland?")

Mystified

Our daughters, Adele and Emma, had begged us to get them a kitten for a Christmas present just before we moved from Tyneside. We already had a much loved and very old dog called Clare. I had my misgivings about acquiring a cat. Particularly as I knew we would soon be moving house and home. But pester power won out as usual, and Jackie brought home a beautiful little kitten on Christmas morning to two delighted and tearful children. Quite how he came by the name Misty is a mystery (see what I did there?). But I really should have realised what lay ahead when I learnt that he hailed from Kenton, Newcastle-upon-Tyne.

Misty settled into life at The Palakona Guest House with impressive ease. We didn't need to butter his paws, not once. He initially provided our guests with great entertainment, running up and down the curtains and annoying the long-suffering dog. Oh, how we all laughed. At least, we did until he began to turn more sinister in his behaviours.

On one occasion, a guest was relaxing in the lounge reading a book, in a world of her own and enjoying her holiday while her hubby was out fishing. She was wearing open-toed sandals, and sat absent-mindedly wriggling her toes as she immersed herself in her novel.

The toe-wriggling action intrigued Misty, who just couldn't resist the urge for a 'kill', and he launched himself at the guest's protruding digits. She shrieked in shock and pain – Misty had drawn blood. We could only apologise profusely and apply first-aid. For some reason this couple never did make a return booking.

Not long after this episode, Jackie saw Misty in the back yard with a bird, still half-alive, in his mouth. She chased after him with a broom in an attempt to persuade him to part with his prey. Misty was having none of it; he ran past her into the house and thence hid in the nearby tumble-dryer. By the time we could persuade him to leave the poor bird alone, it had sadly died. For weeks afterwards the tumble-dryer produced fluffy (and very dry) feathers whenever it was used. I hadn't heard Jackie use such bad language for many a year.

Another one of his favourite tricks was to catch frogs in the garden ponds; he would carefully bring one up to the house, holding it gently in his mouth, then sit and play with it; delicately batting the frog back and forth between his paws as it tried to escape. He would do this repeatedly until he got bored, whereupon he would put the frog back into his mouth and return it from whence it came. He wasn't all bad, I suppose.

Misty's days were numbered, though, when he started sneaking into bedrooms and peeing in corners. It stunk to high heaven – not the best aroma to greet potential guests on being shown around. Twice we had to replace the entire carpet, at some considerable cost. But the final straw was still to come.

Misty Goes In For The Kill

We had a group of anglers from Liverpool staying. Men of varying ages, enjoying a weekend away. Just the kind of client-group we were aiming for. They had finished their evening meal and some were sat watching TV, while others busied themselves upstairs in preparation for a night out in the pubs of Newton Stewart.

I was clearing away their dinner plates, when out of the corner of my eye I spotted Misty in a predatory 'launch' position on the back of the settee. It was one of those moments when your brain is quick enough to tell you what's about to happen, but not quite quick enough to allow you to do anything about it.

Clearly unable to resist his primeval urges, Misty leapt onto the head of one of the sitting guests, snatched what was clearly a toupee, and ran away with it triumphantly to administer the 'kill'. The guest jumped to his feet clutching his scratched pate, swearing and blushing. He didn't blush as much as me.

It took me quite a few moments to locate and retrieve his toupee. Misty, apparently disappointed at the lack of fight in his latest victim, had dropped it in a dark corner and run away to hide.

The guest also ran away, up to his room, leaving his pals in fits of laughter, barely able to breathe as they each in turn re-enacted the scene. Apparently this chap wasn't the most popular member of the club. As one of them said later, "Don't worry about it Ken, it couldn't have happened to a better prat!"

We saw very little of that particular guest throughout the weekend. I didn't have the heart to charge him for his stay.

For Misty though, it was the end of the line. We decided that having a feral cat that attacked guests and peed in the bedrooms wasn't in keeping with our intended corporate image. Misty had to go, and I looked up the phone number of the nearest vet.

Fortunately for Misty, my brother Clive had in-laws who were cat lovers. They already knew Misty and were only too happy to give him a second chance in life. Adele and Emma took this decision very well, realising that he was heading for a life as a spoilt and over-indulged house pet.

Misty became 'Henry', moved to Whitley Bay, and apparently lived happily ever after.

Elsewhere in the World . . .

Meanwhile, in a world that increasingly passed us by, the then British Gas chairman was given a 66 per cent pay increase (some things never change), Boris Yeltsin became the first popularly elected Russian president, and Maggie Thatcher announced her retirement from the Commons. "One of her wiser judgements," said Labour leader, Neil Kinnock.

War was rife in the world, as ever, with Ulster, Iraq and the Balkans scenes of armed and bloody conflicts.

In music, Cher topped the UK charts with 'The Shoop Shoop Song' and REM sang about 'Shiny Happy People', while the same year saw the start of 'Have I Got News for You' on television, and Jack Dee won the British Comedy Award for 'Best Newcomer'.

Little wonder, really, that I spent most of my time familiarising myself with my new business and very little time in front of the television.

Meanwhile back in my world of mud and midges a diary entry in July read:

> *Boat baled out but still leaks. Terrible twins came claiming half the day ticket income. Carp seen cruising and cavorting in the weeds but still not caught. Jim the carpenter has completed the bridge over the weir. Day tickets selling well.*
> *I got smashed up by a large carp on peg one on the island, using sweet corn on 4lb line, tench fishing.*

The boat in question was supposedly part of the business assets that had been included in the purchase. The previous owner informed me that it was originally a rowing boat from Scarborough boating lake. When I inherited it, the boat lay upside-down and partly-submerged, looking like a floundering wooden whale. The rowlocks were missing, as were the oars, the seats were water sodden, and there was no anchor. Some business asset this was.

I managed to lasso the distressed monster, and drag it to the side for a closer inspection. Pulling it on to dry land and turning it over left me utterly exhausted. It was clinker built, of solid and stable wooden construction, ideal as a work boat, and vital to my needs. Unfortunately, it took in water like a sponge. My amateurish attempts at repairs merely made things worse. I left it out of the water to dry out. Big mistake. I caulked it with window sealant. Another big mistake. I bought the wrong rowlocks. But how was I to know they came in different sizes? While the paddles I picked up on the cheap barely moved the boat along at all, the slightest breeze would see me moving in the opposite direction, despite rowing frantically like Hiawatha. There was no manual for such things, you know?

Eventually I cut my losses, and accepted that this boat would leak no matter what I did to try and repair it. I would leave it tied up, and bale it out if and when I needed to use the damn thing. Baling out took so long, and the boat was so heavy to manoeuvre even after all that effort, I used it only sparingly. My back and I were delighted when Andrew Gladstone, the estate owner, eventually purchased a modern work-boat that he kindly allowed me to use.

The Work-Boat RIP; Duly Laid to Rest.

"Show Us the Money"

One morning in July of that first summer, I was sat in the kitchen of the Palakona enjoying a well-earned cup of coffee when the doorbell rang. Two clearly agitated men let themselves in, bursting through the front door. Clearly angry, they both bore stout walking sticks and were accompanied by equally agitated dogs, barking and yapping, and pulling on the leads. They confronted me angrily, shouting in coarse

Yorkshire accents, "We've come for our Craichlaw money and don't mess us about." When I professed my ignorance as to neither what on earth they were talking about nor even who they were, they became even more intimidatory and belligerent. They bellowed at me, "Don't come the clever shite with us pal, pay up or you'll regret it!"

Now I am inherently a fairly placid fellow, apart from when playing football. It normally takes a lot to get me angry. But on this occasion I was instantly furious. Who the hell were these two pricks to come marching into my home uninvited, demanding money with menaces? But I was new in town, and these two looked like they could turn nasty at any moment, as could their dogs. The kids were at school but my wife, Jackie, was present. Should I turn *her* loose on them, I wondered? It hardly seemed fair. After all, there were only two of them, plus dogs. Despite these difficult circumstances I decided that that it would be a bit over the top, even for these two cowboys.

No, I had to play things cool and use my mental health nursing skills to calm all of us down and diffuse the whole situation in order to establish some facts. Eventually, I was able to discover that this was yet another aspect of the business we had bought into that the previous owner had failed to disclose to us. Apparently, he had entered into an agreement with these two charmers that involved paying them 50 per cent of all day ticket sales. What they provided in return wasn't made clear; perhaps it was heavy-handed bailiffing, judging by their manner.

I explained that my agreement was solely with Andrew Gladstone, the loch owner, and not with them. I suggested that they speak to their solicitor and/or the previous owner for any reparation due, but advised that I would not be paying them one penny. They listened, apologised gruffly and reluctantly, then left as abruptly as they had arrived. I never heard from them again.

Now I may have been new to rural affairs, but to me, in any walk of life there are ways and means of going about matters. Marching into a stranger's home, shouting and threatening him and his wife was unacceptable. I doubt they ever did get their money. I hope they didn't, anyway.

Diary entry, August 1991:
Midges are a nuisance! I've repaired or replaced as
many pallets as I can. Kevin has been an immense help.
Hot and sweaty work.
Tench still proving the most caught fish, particularly
dawn and dusk. After dark the dreaded eels appear.
Rhododendrons were cut back where necessary,
especially on the island where pegs one and two were
virtually unfishable.
Day tickets still selling well. Two carp anglers were
smashed up by large carp off peg 6 on the drive. Still
no carp actually landed that I am aware of.
Tested the PH today, a very healthy 6.7. Can't be
accurate, surely?

The Great Escape . . .

One morning as I flung open the door to the outhouse, I found a very large and equally distressed cow staring at me. It was slavering and sweating, with steam rising off its broad back – not dissimilar to me, actually. We were both equally shocked at the confrontation. I wasn't sure what to do next, not having found myself in a situation like this before. I tried whispering in its ear. That didn't work. I waved at it with a handy brush, and managed to gently ease it out of the outhouse and into the yard, where I noticed that it had left generous deposits of that which is reportedly good for the garden all around the car park.

What to do next? I continued to ponder. I could hardly phone the RSPCA, and I didn't think a vet would help. So I phoned the local police station, half expecting them to ask, "But has the cow actually committed any crime, sir?" They were helpful, and didn't seem all that surprised. Presumably, finding a cow in your back garden wasn't unheard of in these rural parts . It transpired that the beast had escaped from the nearby abattoir, launching one final bid for freedom before meeting its maker.

Two chaps promptly arrived, wearing brown coats and carrying stout sticks. They soon persuaded the poor animal back up the alleyway, and off to its doom.

While this incident didn't exactly persuade me to become vegan, I must confess that the Sunday dinner that week didn't have its usual appeal. It was an upsetting outcome for me, and indeed, even more so for the cow.

The abattoir permanently closed down just a short while later.

'Everybody Needs Good Neighbours ... '

It is my belief that in most areas of human enterprise, hard work, ability, diligence and a willingness to take risks are all crucial to success. But above all these, one vital ingredient is necessary ... plain, common, *good luck*.

In terms of neighbours, we were so very lucky. Eric and June were tolerant and welcoming in equal measure. It can't have been easy sharing access, car-parking and a back yard with a busy guest house, and later a tackle shop! The level of activity we generated must have been particularly noticeable given they had become accustomed to the business being quiet. But Eric and June adapted with an equanimity that I doubt I could have mustered had the positions been reversed.

One further stroke of luck we received came our way from June's brother, Kevin. Hailing from Sunderland, he initially came to the area looking for work, and later found long term employment at the local butchers. But while he was on the job hunt, Kev was a Godsend! Ever willing to help, he was the type of person who just could not sit around doing nothing. He was well-built, energetic and powerful, and provided much of the physical labour that was essential in the early days of renovation and rebuilding. Where Eric, who also helped out, and I would share the burden of carrying a heavy pallet, Kevin would easily hoist one on to his shoulder, and pick up one in his other arm! He was a strong lad. Over the next few years he proved to be an invaluable assistant and friend to me as I developed 'Craichlaw Fisheries'. In return, Kev enjoyed free fishing, free transport and all the tackle he needed at cost price. Meanwhile his sister June was grateful that, as she saw it, "You're keeping our Kevin out of mischief."

> *Diary entry, September 1991:*
> *I've finally finished repairing all the pallets and Andrew tells me he intends replacing them with specially constructed dry-stone pegs! While this will undoubtedly improve the appearance of the fishery overall, I really, really wish he had told me of his plans before now!*
> *Day tickets continue to sell well, so well that I'm slightly miffed now. I wished I negotiated a deal with Andrew for 50% of said sales rather than the agreed lease deal.*
> *Tench are feeding freely, the trouble is that when the tench are feeding, so are the midges! Dawn and dusk are always better, however an hour or so after dark and the eels move in.*
> *I watched two large carp cruising around in the shallows. I wonder just how many of them there are in Craichlaw?*

September proved to be a lucrative time of the year for the business as a whole. While the family holidays were over and kids back at school, those of us whose businesses didn't rely on school holiday breaks did well. We found to our pleasant surprise that we were fully booked for lengthy periods of the autumn of 1991. Guests were either more mature couples seeking a quiet break away, or anglers freed from parental duties over the summer school holiday looking to spend time on the bank-side to restore their energy levels and sanity.

Visitors from a Previous Life

During this period, I was delighted to welcome one of the student nurse groups that I'd been teaching in my previous life! It was great to see them all again and to hear their various tales of woe and joy. What a wonderful weekend we enjoyed, they filled the accommodation, meaning that Jackie and I could enjoy their company as they checked out the various pubs in town. We didn't really want to join them, you understand, but felt obliged to do so, in keeping with our role as cordial hosts.

Being Geordies, they mixed freely with the equally friendly locals to the point where a hastily arranged 'students vs locals' football match was organised. The game took place on a pitch in a nearby public park, and involved a lot of falling over, much topping up of alcohol levels as the game progressed, and no one keeping the score. Stupidly, I joined in, and consequently suffered generalised aches and pains for days afterwards. I also remember hearing some dreadful verbal abuse from the touchline!

I was sorry to see them all leave. Some have been in touch more recently via social media, and it is gratifying to hear about the successful careers many of them have enjoyed.

Back To the Day-Job

One September evening, an angler from Glasgow was bivvying at Craichlaw and made the fatal error of not setting up his tackle correctly. Too slow to react when his bite alarm sounded, he had to watch forlornly as his rod, reel and terminal tackle suddenly slithered into the loch, with a large fish attached.

"Camped out for 36 hours, and it was the only f'kin bite I got," he announced, bitterly. I was furious with him, fearing for the welfare of my precious fish. Later that evening he actually watched as his float and rod clearly still attached to a large carp went sailing through his swim! Fortunately for him, and even more for the fish concerned, his quarry managed to somehow shed the entire tackle. Rod, reel and terminal rig, including the hook, were found floating in the shallows the following morning.

The next month was to be an exciting and apprehensive time for my precious fishery, as Andrew revealed plans to drain and dredge the loch. Little did I realise just how ambitious those plans were!

This, our first summer, was proving a real eye-opener for us both. The day tickets sold surprisingly strongly, and the guest house was full on many nights, largely due to passing trade but also as we gradually advertised to expand our angling market.

Craichlaw Loch proved to be popular as a tench fishery and was well known in the coarse angling fraternity, particularly to those anglers that already had visited Dumfries and Galloway. The carp were proving much more elusive, but then I reasoned very few anglers actually fished for them.

I knew before taking on this job that acid rain, and consequentially high levels of acid water levels were a real problem in this heavily forested area of Scotland. To subsequently find that Craichlaw had a PH level of nearly 6.7 (with 7.0 being neutral) was a pleasant, if puzzling, surprise. The explanation became obvious when I discovered mounds of lime around the water's edge, placed there by previous owners in an attempt to redress the acidity problem. This is a common and effective method of introducing lime, allowing it to gradually leach into the water over a long period of time.

As the summer turned toward autumn I continued to watch, listen and learn. Most of all I counted my blessings that *this*, yes *this* was my job, my means of earning a living, how I paid the mortgage and put food on the table. I was loving every minute of it.

Changes

Diary entry, October 1991:
Loch renovation projects commenced! A cut was made with a digger into the bank by peg 21 and an outlet stream created down to the burn and thence into the river Tarff. What started off as a gentle trickle of water soon turned into a raging torrent as it cascaded down the bank-side and into the burn.
We lowered the levels by two and a half feet. Quite amazing watching the changes as the life blood of the loch gushed away. The fish went scatty!! Large carp

were pushing around the reed fringes frantically looking for 'home!' The roach and rudd clung together around the potamogeton weed beds in shoals of dashing, jumping and clearly distressed fish.

Overgrown lily-beds that were previously inaccessible are now reachable by very careful wading. Very deep silt, particularly at the boat-house end of the loch was exposed. I started to cut two pegs that Andrew went on to clear with the digger. We gave up on two pegs but opened up two more. The slime and filth, while an undoubted attraction for the fish, absolutely stinks, harbouring bloodworm and midges.

The digger arrived one day and broke down the next, it took a week to repair it. Work finished to all intents and purposes within three weeks. However, tidying up and construction of the dry-stone platforms is taking much longer. My initial concerns were unfounded, all the fish seem to have survived well, no casualties discovered. Now the real work begins.

Local joiner, Jim Montgomery, has built a new bridge across to the island. It looks beautiful, just like Monet's 'Water Lilies' painting. I suggested that we leave one side without a rail to allow anglers to carry their gear across more easily and Andrew kindly agreed.'

The decision to de-silt and clean out Craichlaw Loch was an arbitrary one, made by Andrew apparently some time before I took over the fishing rights. He had mentioned it during our initial negotiations, but I hadn't noted any clear dates and inexplicably attached little importance to the idea, so when it did happen it came as a shock!

Not many anglers get to see the bottom of the waters they fish, except perhaps in extreme drought conditions, and even then it is a gradual process. To expose weed beds, lily pads, the original river-bed and favourite fish holding areas, all in a sudden 48-hour period was quite unnerving, for me as well as for the fish! In one area, mounds of untouched ground bait, introduced by a group of match-anglers a few days before, suddenly reappeared, like cakes spoiled in the rain, sitting atop mounds of slimy silt . . . it was utterly surreal.

The whole process gave me the opportunity to create swims where none had previously existed, and to reclaim those that had vanished beneath a jungle of lilies and weeds. It was a one-off opportunity, and one that I valued highly. I intended to make the most of it and spent hours poring over maps and charts, then explaining these plans with Andrew and the digger driver to ensure that clearances occurred where I wanted them. This chance to create what would be an almost new fishery while retaining the best virtues of the original one was near unique, yet it was one I knew I was largely unqualified to make the most of. Who was I, to undertake such an operation? I wasn't particularly proficient at catching fish, let alone creating sound, healthy environments in which they would thrive.

A drained and forlorn-looking Craichlaw Loch looking toward the Boat House, 1991 – same view as earlier photograph.

Fortunately, I was prepared to some extent by my previous experience in academia. This wasn't an academic assignment marked against established criteria. My family and I were to live or die on my ability to make a success out of this change of life. I had to have a reasonably in-depth knowledge of the subject. Lacking much experience on maintaining a fishery, I turned to the literature to learn as much as I could; the following reading list is the outcome of my research, and if formed the basis for my ongoing fishery management:

A Fishery of Your Own, Rickards B. and Whitehead K., published by A&C Black (1984)

Management of Coarse Fishing Waters, Birch E., published by John Baker (1964)

Fishery Management, Institute of Fisheries Management, (Article, source and date obscure)

Textbook of Fish Culture, Breeding and Cultivation of Fish, Marcel Huet, published by Fishing News Books Ltd (1972)

Creating Your Own Fishery, Marlborough D., (Article, source and date obscure)

I also sought out the advice of whatever local specialist input was available, both anecdotal and scientific. The latter was specifically provided courtesy of the local fisheries scientific officer, Dr Alistair Stephens, who provided friendly, practical and evidence-based advice, the former from local anglers, particularly my old friend Tony Taylor, more of whom later.

Diary entry November 1991:
Water levels in Craichlaw still well down, I'm a bit worried about this. Also a cormorant is getting good and fat on my fish! I was led to believe by Dave Canning that it could be shot under licence, not so . . . each case apparently has to be demonstrated to be 'causing serious economic hardship.'
Sad news, our tame duck, Albert, has been shot. I bet he walked right up to the gun barrel expecting tit-bits from humans just as he has for years. He was so tame, who the hell would want to shoot him?
I'll continue the process of introducing lime into the burn and at points around the loch-side.

Winter draws on . . . literally. Although South West Scotland enjoys a largely temperate climate, bathed as it is by the Gulf Stream, the onset of winter meant a sharp learning curve for those of trying to make a living from a tourist related business. To many in the UK the image of a Scottish winter is one of snow, ice and grey skies. While Dumfries and Galloway certainly lived up to the stereotype with regard to the latter, the former is not too common. Temperatures usually hover between eight and 12 degrees Celsius from November to March, but we needed to convince folk that pike fishing, wildfowling and other country sports, including cycling, golf and hill walking were both possible and enjoyable during our winter. Even the carp and tench would feed sporadically, but how could we attract guests throughout winter?

4 THAT FIRST WINTER . . .

> *Diary entry, December 1991:*
> *Bleak! The loch is now completely refilled, only to*
> *promptly flood. Occasional repairs needed to some of*
> *the newly constructed stone pegs. A few roach coming*
> *out but little else . . .*

A short diary entry indeed, thus indicating the level of angling activity at Craichlaw that first winter.

Meanwhile, as a family we had to adapt to a new life in a new town and a new country. Work on the guest house continued, albeit taking one step forward and two back at times. The absence of a Fire Certificate meant that we couldn't open the upstairs bedrooms for accommodation, thus losing much needed income. We had to sacrifice the family lounge for guest use, leaving us with a derelict large lounge devoid of heating and decoration.

Jackie and kids keeping warm, Christmas 1991.

The Fire Officer had asked us to remove the wooden panelling in the hall, stairs and middle landing in order to further fireproof these areas. In so doing, we discovered a hall doorway behind the panelling that had been filled in with timber at some point in the past. This doorway had to be bricked up and made fire resistant. Even the stairs were deemed to be unsafe, and had to be replaced. Things were not going to plan.

Any romantic notions that may have ever been held regarding this lifestyle change were disappearing as rapidly as the sleet, snow and slush outside. We'd anticipated this first winter being difficult, but we hadn't expected to have to have a guest house like a building site and potential guests wary to book.

Family and friends joined us for the New Year's Festivities, providing some cheer and good humour. We needed it. Our friends from Tyneside and a great many locals saw to it that our first Hogmanay was one to remember . . . except I can't! I do remember the hangover. No wonder January 2nd is a public holiday in Scotland, or 'Recovery Day', as it is known locally.

When everyone had left we felt all the more isolated, and I was questioning whether the entire idea was a disaster that needed to be rectified as soon as possible.

We needed patience, faith in our abilities, and an upturn in trade. Relief came from an unexpected source . . .

The Shooting Fraternity; a strange breed indeed
We were gradually encouraged by the number of wildfowlers ringing up looking for accommodation. The Palakona had been a favourite base for wildfowlers and deer stalkers in the past, but trade had fallen away over recent years, and we had no expectation that they would return. Thankfully, word soon got out in the shooting fraternity that new owners had taken over, and guest house bookings began to improve rapidly. Thank God, as there was precious little other trade around at the time.

I had a moral dilemma, however. I wasn't too keen on the whole idea of shooting animals just for fun, but if the sport were to bring enough trade to the guest house to keep the business afloat, then who was I to turn it away? I rationalised that the shooters would only stay elsewhere, while the same animals and birds would be shot, so why not? Call me superficial, but I had a family to care for. I also really should have thought this through before buying a business that relied on such trade . . . D'oh!

By and large the shooters that we entertained were an amiable lot, with some strange ones amongst them, of course. I suppose that any sport requiring you to get out of a warm bed and leave your partner in the early hours of a Scottish winter's morning to go and lie full length in a sea of mud will attract a few odd-bods.

As guests, shooters proved easy to please. I built kennels in the rear outbuildings, and placed large bales of straw for their dogs to sleep in. Silly me – virtually all of the dogs slept in the bedroom with their masters, with some ON the beds, judging by the amount of dog hair we had to clear up. The shooters enjoyed a drink in the local pubs, but having to get up early they were rarely out late.

The wildfowlers would go out onto the marshes, while the deer stalkers and rough shooters went up onto the hills, all at silly o'clock in the morning, then return for breakfast at a reasonable time. Sometimes the deer stalkers would bring their breakfast with them – deer liver. Usually still warm, and sometimes still throbbing, this wasn't something Jackie found easy to prepare! It proved to be one of the few occasions on which I had to take over cooking duties.

The entries the shooters left in the guest-book read like a foreign language to me. Comments such as 'Finally got a pinkie under the moon,' or 'Loads of greys off the Bishop's burn,' left me pondering what it all meant. I didn't like to reveal my ignorance by asking. After due consideration, I felt obliged to join a group of wildfowlers and experience their sport for myself, in the hope that I could appreciate just what it was that attracted them to it in the first place. I arose from my nice warm bed and sleeping wife at 5:30 a.m. on a cold, dark and bleak January morning. I wrapped up warm, made a flask of coffee, grabbed an oilcloth to lie on and set off with big Kevin and his pals from Leicestershire.

A short drive of ten minutes or so took us to a favoured access point at Wigtown Bay, where public wildfowling was permitted. We slithered and splashed our way across the merse, through ditches and culverts, clambering over barbed wire fences, risking castration in so doing. It was more tiring and dangerous than I'd anticipated, particularly in the pitch dark with just torches to guide us. I realised that we had to be wary of the incoming tide on our return journey, too.

Having found a suitable spot to hunker down, we all split up and readied ourselves. I must admit that there was a very real sense of being at one with nature. My guests all vanished, camouflaged so perfectly it was impossible to pick them out, even with my binoculars. Evidently the wildlife were equally oblivious to our presence, because as I lay in the ditch I could hear various wildfowl calling, and seagulls screeching overhead.

A splashing in the nearby burn drew my attention. It was an otter making his way upstream – hopefully not to Craichlaw Loch, I recall thinking at the time. As the mists rose and the sky began to clear ever so slightly, a large red fox ambled his way across the mud flats. If he only knew that he was in front of a dozen primed and ready shotguns! I suspect at some point he must have picked up our scent, or at least that of the dogs, as he abruptly picked up his pace and left our vicinity quite briskly.

Eventually, a whisper came from an invisible person to my right. "Get down, keep still, don't move a muscle. They're coming in . . . " Sure enough, a pair of Greylag geese circled overhead, and having scouted the area, eventually landed. A few more followed, and then a few more, until the sky was full of geese, all honking and squawking in unison. It was quite exciting. Shots began to ring out from the various points where our guests and other shooters had placed themselves. Many, many more shots followed, until the geese wheeled away up into the sky, landing further away out at sea or out of range of the slowly quietening guns.

Faithful dogs were sent to retrieve the shot geese – brave, well trained and fearless animals they were, too. They leapt through mud, ditch and foam to grasp their prey gently but firmly, and dropped them at their master's feet. Some of the dead geese had fallen into the sea, but this meant little to a determined retriever; indeed, sometimes the dog's owner would have to whistle the dog back to safety, as it went into deeper and deeper water where the swirling tide and currents would have made retrieval very dangerous.

I drank my coffee in readiness to make the trek back to the vehicles and warmth. But no . . . we were to all hide back down in our foxholes, and wait. Sure enough, another wave of geese came in. Skein after skein of them, the noise was incredible. You literally had to be there to believe it. Another barrage of shots rang out, lasting ten minutes or so. The dogs were sent on their retrieval missions again, until a loud voice announced the end of the shoot as the tide advanced rapidly.

We couldn't retrace our footsteps as the sea had filled in much of the route we'd taken. I was pleased I was with folk who knew their way across this increasingly dangerous terrain. Where were those deep culverts? Where were those barbed-wire fences? The thought of being out here alone mortified me. How many wildfowlers hadn't made it back over the years? I wondered .

Eventually we made it to the vehicles, where we scraped off as much of the Solway mud as possible from ourselves and the dogs before heading home, where Jackie would have a hot and sorely need breakfast ready.

I noticed just how devoted the wildfowlers were to their dogs. They would hose them down and feed them, settling them into the relative warmth of the kennels before even entering the guest house to see to their own needs.

Wildfowlers, rear of Palakona.

Afterwards, I found it rather disturbing to realise that I could actually begin to understand the appeal of the sport. You certainly communed with nature in a very real manner. Man against the elements, the terrain, the prey and all that existential stuff. It was harsh and bleak. I reluctantly had to concede that the whole experience appealed to a previously unrecognised part of my hunter-gatherer self.

But I still baulked at the actual killing part of the experience. The geese weren't needed for food. Had we been shooting with a camera I would've been much more likely to take up the sport.

Diary entry, February 1992:
Craichlaw Loch bank-side continues to look like a bomb-site.
I trimmed bushes and trees from the bank-side. The silt and mud removed from the bottom of the loch as a result of all the renovation work has been spread around the immediate environs in huge amounts. In truth it looks like a World War I battlefield.
Large amounts of dead reeds and weeds formed vast rafts of heavy and hard to move debris around the margins. I've been laboriously dragging it all in and piling it up at the side of the loch but Andrew has asked me to hide it around the base of bank-side rhododendrons as the large piles appeared 'unsightly'.

The Cormorant has returned but is much more nervous, having somehow survived the presence of shooters on the loch over the early Winter. Nobody is fishing the place; even I can only manage small bags of roach or rudd and the odd perch.

Craichlaw Loch, moonscape banks, Jan, 1992,
post dredging and levels back up.

It was time to turn my attention elsewhere . . .

Silver Bars

The River Cree runs directly through the heart of Newton Stewart and immediately to the rear of our guest house. In the past it had enjoyed a reputation for wonderful salmon fishing, with large runs of fresh run salmon and sea-trout. Unfortunately the Cree's glory days were behind it by the time we arrived. Nevertheless, it remained a popular spate-river destination for salmon anglers, and when I first started fishing in the area I had a go at fishing for them.

This involved paying a substantial amount to either join the local angling association or to purchase a day-ticket. It also meant slowly but surely fishing each pool, regularly changing leader, fly or both. I found the constant casting required irritated a long-standing neck condition, while the midges were an absolute menace – they were hard to brush off with both hands full of tackle. I also found the treacherous conditions underfoot difficult to master. I could frequently be seen stumbling and splashing around, much to the amusement of the watching local anglers. I was very good at catching though, even if I say so myself. I caught gorse bushes, bank-side cages and tree branches. I actually caught a traffic cone once, and the cap of a fellow angler waiting to fish the pool that I was lashing into a froth. I spent hours and hours trudging up and down the river, forlornly hoping that something, anything would take my fly. I latched into a powerful fish on one occasion; *something to brag about at last*, I thought. Silly me. The salmon took off down the river, heading for Wigtown at a hundred miles an hour. It shed the hook, leaving me devastated and out of breath. My feet ached, my back was sore and my pride was hurt beyond repair. I decide that salmon fishing perhaps just wasn't for me.

The author with both a mullet and a salmon 1992.

PIKE!

It was winter in Scotland, and we were based in one the most prolific areas of the UK for pike angling. I had planned for a much greater uptake of pike anglers in the first year's accommodation business plan than we were experiencing. This was yet another unforeseen problem for me to have to reconcile.

I had fished many of the local pike waters myself frequently over the years. I realised, though, that such fishing trips were far less common during the winter months. Pike angling was for the most part less of a group activity, where match anglers would travel in significant numbers to fish club competitions. Pike anglers preferred to travel and fish alone, or in pairs at most. (Having said that, I soon came to learn that the local pike anglers did enjoy competitions, but sadly, being local, they didn't need accommodation. They did need bait, however, and often tackle too . . . A light bulb moment flashed in my mind, more of which later.)

We certainly needed to advertise for pike anglers, and I needed to be able to provide them with the advice they'd need for an enjoyable stay. Advertising proved expensive, and brought only a trickle of a response. The acquisition of local knowledge, on the other hand, was time consuming but more enjoyable.

Wherever I've been fishing in the world, I've always 'asked the locals'. This policy has usually paid dividends. (Although that time in Bulgaria was interesting. They didn't speak English and I couldn't speak Bulgarian, but hey . . . I still caught carp.) So here on my own doorstep, I set about doing the same thing, asking the following set of questions:

* Which waters had a reputation for pike fishing?
* Who controlled the fishing rights, where could you purchase permits, and at what price?
* Who controlled access to the water's edge, and from which access point?
* Was vehicular access good? (Coarse anglers took a *lot* of tackle, some were reputedly sponsored by kitchen sink manufacturers Armitage Shanks.)
* Under what conditions did the water fish best?
* What swims were most productive, and when?
* What baits worked best: dead baits, popped up, jerked, static on the bottom, spinning, plug or spoon, etc?
* What rules were in place? Live-baiting was always contentious, and how about the use of barbless trebles, overnight bivvying, 'No Fires', keep-nets, landing mats etc?

I was very quickly reminded that fishing is all about opinions! Many responses were contrary, some just untrue, and sadly, some were intentionally misleading.

One of the most helpful sources of local information was Richard Thornton, the son of the previous owner. Richard knew the local pike waters well, and had always been helpful in the past whenever I had called in for a day ticket. He had briefly run a tackle shop in what had been the lounge of our guest house, as well.

Pike Problem? Solution, and Sabotage . . .

Sabotage usually came from the anti-pike brigade, whose mantra was, 'The only good pike is a dead pike.' Many of those people controlling game fishing waters insisted that all pike were to be removed. Indeed, this was invariably written into the rules.

On one occasion, the Scottish representative of the Pike Angling Club (PAC) and I gave a talk to the local game angling association. We presented the scientific-based evidence that the existence of pike in trout waters was beneficial for a healthy trout population. While those present at the meeting were courteous and polite, and most of the committee members seemed convinced by the science, I'm afraid that the members continued to kill all pike caught. They complained that their waters held large numbers of hungry, small pike and that these were decimating the trout stocks. Yet they continued to remove the larger pike, the one predator that would have kept the numbers of small pike and ailing trout in check.

However, we did establish a tentative and mutually beneficial agreement to fish a local trout water renowned for the large number of sizeable pike it held. The agreement reached was that a series of pike fishing matches could be held on the understanding that all pike over 6lb caught would be held in netted holding cages, then transferred to a nearby pike water. Pike under 6lb were to be humanely dispatched.

We advertised this opening event widely and sold many day tickets; we also had a guest house full of excited anglers. On arrival at the venue, Ochiltree Loch, on the morning of the first competition, we found to our horror and fury that almost all the cages had been vandalised, destroyed beyond repair. Pike anglers had travelled considerable distances, from places as far afield as Cumbria, Tyneside and Glasgow. They'd made this trek, some staying overnight in local accommodation, on the strict understanding that no pike over 6lb would be killed. Through gritted teeth, I had to explain to these anglers at registration that the whole project had been sabotaged. Furthermore, the committee members of the controlling angling association present were insisting that if I had no means to hold and transfer the larger pike as agreed, then they also *must* be killed. On hearing this most of the pike anglers simply cursed and drove away to fish alternative local venues where such outdated and primitive practices were banned.

This debacle proved to be the end of any attempts on my part to help the local angling association with their perceived 'pike problem'. The 'Fluff-Flingers' and the 'Maggot Munchers' maintained social distancing between each other thereafter.

One local trout angler, Andy Johnstone, landed a 32lb specimen pike while fishing for trout on fly gear using 6lb breaking-strain line. This was from the nearby angling association trout water, Fyntalloch Loch. Quite an accomplishment in terms of angling skill, but somewhat spoilt, in my opinion, by crushing the old lady's skull with a rock on landing her. He brought the fish round to show me (see photo) and seemed surprised when I declined the offer to buy it from him with a view to having it stuffed and mounted.

Now, Andy is a friendly enough chap and an excellent game angler. We got on well enough at the time, and still do. He did what he felt was the right thing to do for his sport. But it demonstrated forcibly to me just how deeply felt and firmly entrenched these anti-pike feelings were. Of course, it is difficult to try to hold the moral high ground when we all cause fish distress in enjoying our sport, whether we kill them or not, so I won't attempt to do so here.

The author with Andy Johnstone's 32lb Pike from Fyntalloch Loch;
Caught on 6lb line fly-fishing but then dispatched.

Ice Age Errors

Not all local anglers were anti-pike. Indeed, there were enough local pike anglers to form a coarse angling club in the area. Consisting of perhaps 20 or so members, we would meet in the Palakona Guest House to discuss issues, swap stories and arrange competitions. This proved a rich source of material for me as I set about my familiarisation with local waters.

But the best way to learn, in my view, is experientially. Get out there and do it; experience it. Based on this premise, Kev and I visited just about every pike water in the vicinity, from Loch Maben near Dumfries, where I had more success with nocturnal bream than pike, to Clatteringshaws Dam, Loch Heron and Loch Maberry.

I was pleased that Kev had found work in 'Owens', the local butchers, (where he still works to this day). However, it did limit the opportunities for him to accompany me fishing, meaning that many of my trips went ahead on a solo basis. I didn't really mind; as I've previously stated I quite enjoyed my own company, certainly often better than other people enjoy my company.

One exploratory trip when Kev did accompany me was to Loch Maberry, just on the border with South Ayrshire and well known to the local pike angling fraternity. Maberry was an under-fished pike water; at least, this was the case for the East bank, where we intended fishing.

It was a bitterly cold January morning, with a milder Westerly front only very gradually thawing out the local lochs following a lengthy cold snap. Iced up waters meant fishing had been impossible for a long time, and we were desperate. Snow and sleet showers greeted us as we set off, more in hope than expectation.

As we neared the loch it initially appeared still to be frozen solid, but we were optimistic that the bay we intended fishing might be clear, as local anglers had suggested might be the case. The approach involved a lengthy walk from the car park/lay-by, down a steep incline to the water's edge. We were relieved to see moving water and small waves as we arrived. At last . . . somewhere to fish!

The strenuous descent, conducted while loaded up with tackle, meant that I was lathered in sweat on arrival at the water-side. I was wearing a set of thermals plus a thick 'Teddy' undersuit and an all-weather waterproof jacket on top; I was prepared for the cold, but I also retained the sweat, keeping me cold and damp.

Kev and I set up our swims some 100 yards apart, to improve the chances of locating the fish. Having briefly plumbed bottom, and finding the weed-beds surprisingly shallow, we put out three rods each at various distances and with different dead baits, again to improve the odds of success. Just for interest, smelt, mackerel, eel and herring were favourites. Some of our baits were anchored hard on the bottom, some popped up mid-water with foam inserts and one I occasionally twitched very gently with my Jerk rod outfit. Two hours later, and I still had nothing. Not a take, a run, a surface swirl or even a gentle enquiry; it was the same for Kev.

As I sat, bored and shivering, I realised that I'd left my flask of coffee in the car and, feeling the desperate need for a warm up, I began the slow and laborious trudge up the steep incline back to the car.

As I made my way back down with coffee flask in hand I paused, out of breath and needing a fag. I looked out across the bay we were fishing. It was a stunning view; a wild Scottish landscape at its most attractive. I spotted Kev hunched over his peg, trying to keep warm, then, from my high vantage point, something else caught my eye. There, directly in front of his margin rod was what looked like a very fishy shaped outline. I made use of the ever present binoculars around my neck, and looked closer. It was indeed a fish, only very small, but a fish at least! As I searched around the immediate area of Kev's swim I noticed another fish further out. A steady and careful study of my swim also revealed two or three very small fish lurking in the area. This was exciting. If there were small jacks or feed fish in the vicinity, then the bigger pike wouldn't be far away – pike are reputedly notorious cannibals. I shouted to Kev and used sign language to tell him that I could see fish right in front of him.

But something about the fish I could see through the binoculars raised my suspicions. Big old queens had learnt the value of ambush techniques, but small young jacks I usually found to always be active, predatory and utterly unable to lie still for any length of time, even in cold water.

I went further down the loch-side, losing the benefit of height but getting closer. I paused again and using my binoculars, zoomed in on these static fish. There had been no change whatsoever; they remained in the precise location I'd first spotted them.

The penny dropped.

I was fairly certain about what I was seeing, and to confirm my suspicions I shouted to Kev, telling him to bring in any of his baits and promising I'd explain why later.

Sure enough, as he reeled in, one of the 'fish' I was watching started moving too, fastened to the end of Kev's line. The fish I could see were our dead-baits! How embarrassing was that?

In the low light of dawn, we had both enthusiastically cast out into open and apparently ice-free but weedy water. We thought that the obvious lack of depth was due to the died-back weed beds into which we had intentionally placed our baits. But no . . .

What we had actually done was to line up all our tempting offerings on top of a huge sheet of crystal clear, thick and impenetrable ice, with about eight inches of melt water lying above – just enough to hide the baits from our view at the bank-side. Little wonder we'd had no bites, then, and that when we'd inspected our baits they appeared completely untouched.

Crestfallen, embarrassed, humiliated and cold, Kev and I packed up and came home. We agreed not to mention this episode of angling idiocy to a living soul, ever.

I certainly haven't . . . until now, when I broadcast it, with names and details in a book.

Sorry, Kev, but with hindsight it was a lesson in acquired angling humility!

Kev Birch, on a more successful day, Loch Heron 19lb 6oz.

Networking and a Lesson in Back-Scratching . . .

Meanwhile, back at The Palakona Guest House things were very slowly improving. We had eventually gained use of the main lounge, allowing the guests to use this and ourselves as a family to finally have some privacy in the small lounge.

In an effort to establish myself and the business within the local community I found myself being forced to spend increasing amounts of time mixing with new-found acquaintances and neighbours, building up a network of contacts and friendships. The best type of environment in which to undertake this onerous task was undoubtedly one of the local pubs, which particularly in these early months meant

The Black Horse Hotel. I shouldered the burden stoically, and without complaint.

Most of the locals were really friendly and welcoming – not all of them, of course, but the vast majority. In the pub we shared common interests in football, fishing, and the question of when the tourist trade would pick up.

I remember complaining to anyone who'd listen just how stupid it was for the Forestry Commission (FC) to sell permits to fish their various waters, only to block access to said waters by padlocking the gates on the access roads. One group of our guests had faced an unexpected mile long trek with all their tackle to reach the loch-side as a result of one of these incidents. They were not a happy bunch of anglers on returning for their evening meal, with backs aching and blisters blooming, vowing never to return. I mentioned the incident one night in the pub to a particular drinking buddy. The next day a FC master key came into my possession, as if by magic!

There was of course an unspoken agreement that such favours were a two-way affair, and a few weeks later and with no notice, we found ourselves child-minding the key donor's young children all day.

Spring 1992

As spring approached, both passing and short-stay trade improved. Our Visitors Book showed guests from diverse parts of the world, including Norway, London and Blackpool.

We also picked up a lot of late-night trade heading to or from the Irish Ferry. Many of these guests were traditional Irish farmers, horse traders or sometimes travellers, but invariably they came with large families. Dad would ring our doorbell, negotiate a price per room in a broad Irish brogue I barely understood, then signal to a parked up vehicle for the family to come and join him. I would stand watching in amazement as first Mum, then a veritable troop of children – all very well behaved – would file in, greeting us with a polite "Hello, and thank you." It was like watching the Von Trapp Family from *The Sound of*

Music or the Tombliboos from the CBBC programme *The Night Garden!* Quite how they managed to accommodate a family of two adults and eight children in a room with three single beds I never knew.

I could usually tell the dealers by the size of the rolled-up wad of money from which payment was taken, and I shuddered at the thought of them losing it or it being stolen. Honestly, those rolls must have consisted of thousands of pounds of notes.

These guests often left very early, at five or six in the morning, passing on the offer of a cooked breakfast. We would leave them a packed breakfast instead, especially for the kids. They were always quiet, well behaved and left the rooms in immaculate condition. Many returned frequently, though they hardly ever phoned in advance. It was heart-breaking to have to deny the familiar cheery faces accommodation when we had no spare rooms.

Diary Entry, March 1992:
General tidying up continues. All the peg number plates are painted and nailed onto wooden stakes. Rather small I think but they may just do the job. Great interest from Glasgow match anglers, best bag was only 3lb of roach and rudd but the loch didn't do itself justice, water temp too low.
Still no sign of the water lilies nor the reed mace re-growing. I'm concerned that draining the water may have disrupted their normal growth cycle?
I have finally managed to stem the leak in the workboat. It still needs a lot of attention AND lifting clear of the water for further maintenance.
I started stocking Spa Wood loch with brown trout taken from Craichlaw Loch.
Let down by another carp dealer again.

Diary Entry, April 1992:
I attended the Angling '92 Exhibition at 'The National
Exhibition Centre' (NEC) Birmingham. Excellent show,
very busy indeed, I ran out of brochures!
Increasing signs of life at Craichlaw! The tench are
feeding with roach and rudd coming out in greater
numbers and size.

In an effort to boost trade and broaden our market appeal we had joined the local Dumfries and Galloway Tourist Board. Access to their marketing literature was useful, as was advertising in the local tourist board information centres where many visitors called in to arrange accommodation.

Unfortunately we were not made very welcome by the ladies manning these centres. One of them told us that she had heard unfavourable reports of The Palakona Guest House in the past and just couldn't bring herself to recommend it to potential visitors.

"Coarse Anglers? Coarse by name, coarse by nature is what I think," she harrumphed, with a supercilious smile.

While part of me secretly agreed with her assessment of certain coarse anglers, it wasn't her place to make such judgements. She and I had an argument while stood in the shop surrounded by visitors. Eventually I phoned her line manager, and as a result we did gradually receive a trickle of trade from the visitor centre.

Being members of the tourist board gave us access to grant aid for marketing and publicity, and it was this that saw me travel down to The National Exhibition Centre (NEC) in Birmingham. Despite the entire visit being partly subsidised it still cost us a small fortune for one stall measuring two metres long by 1.5 metres deep.

Anglers from all over the UK congregated at the NEC in huge numbers. I was staggered by the sheer volume of people! The leaflets, brochures and various handouts were snaffled up rapidly, to the point where I had to ration them, distributing them only to anglers who actually stopped to discuss what we had to offer.

Stand at NEC Angling Exhibition.

I had travelled down with the Tourist Board Regional Manager and the proprietor of a nearby country hotel that also offered fishing holidays. His name was Dave Canning (RIP), and over the years we developed a cautious but mutually beneficial relationship, well sort of.

That night, Dave and I shared a twin room in a nearby hotel. His snoring was so loud that I eventually gave up shouting and throwing shoes at him and simply vacated the room. I set up base in the shared bathroom down the corridor where I locked the door and slept fitfully in a bath with a dripping tap. Such fun . . .

> *Diary Entry, April 1992:*
> *Stocking! Craichlaw stocked with 100 carp . . .*

I had taken advantage of the fact I was heading to Birmingham, by arranging to collect some carp from a dealer based in Worcestershire while I was at the exhibition. He met me in the car park of the NEC, where he handed over a number of poly-bags filled with oxygen rich air and a small amount of water. The fish were a mixture of commons, mirrors and ghost carp, all around the 8-10 inch size.

They all travelled back well with no fatalities, though a few had small netting/handling sores that I treated with Methyline Blue. I introduced them very slowly into Craichlaw Loch later that evening, where they all skipped away with an obvious sense of freedom. They were caught regularly all summer, but sadly very few over-wintered.

> *Diary Entry, April 1992:*
> *Cormorant is back, bastard!*
> *Club trip from Burscough fished Craichlaw but it fished*
> *badly with only 4lb of roach winning the match.*
> *This evening two Scouse lads fished it and had two*
> *roach over 1lb each, typical! (and I forgot my camera.)*
> *Next morning four remaining Burscough lads did much*
> *better with tench to 3lb and plenty of good-sized*
> *roach.*

The spring catch returns from Craichlaw continued with inconsistent weights. The cormorant was a nuisance, taking many fish right in front of my eyes too, cheeky sod. Oh, for a shotgun . . .

It was clear that putting all our fish eggs in the one basket of Craichlaw Loch was not going to work. I needed a wider variety of fishing opportunities for guests to be directed to when Craichlaw wasn't fishing well.

5 DEVELOPMENTS

Everything Comes To He Who Waits . . .

Immediately across the road from Craichlaw Loch and in the same estate grounds lay Glendarroch Loch. This was a small 2.5 acre water that I had previously fished for years, catching quality sized roach and rudd up to 2lb. It had also held bream and tench in the past. Unfortunately, a year or so before we negotiated the deal to buy The Palakona Guest House and lease the fishing rights to Craichlaw Loch, Glendarroch Loch was leased out to a local hotel owner, Bob. Bob had visions of attracting guests to his hotel/pub in the nearby village of Kirkcowan by offering private fishing for trout.

To this end, he drained the loch down, leaving just a very small area of residual water. Bob netted and removed as many of the coarse fish as he could, and set about using a digger to remove as much of the silt, lilies and weeds as possible. He left the loch empty for months, then sealed off the outlet and left it to gradually refill for a year or so before finally stocking it with rainbow trout.

Sadly for Bob but fortuitously for me, his plans proved unsuccessful. The roach, rudd, perch, bream and even the tench had not only survived but bred rapidly and in great numbers. The lilies soon started to flourish again, invading the open water and thereby eventually making fly-fishing virtually impossible.

The upshot all of this was that Bob relinquished the lease, and Mr

Gladstone offered it to me. Guess who was delighted?

Although very shallow and weedy, requiring huge amounts of time and effort to keep it fishable, I knew that this was one of the alternative fishing venues I'd been seeking.

> *Diary Entry, May 1992:*
> *Swim-cutting continues on Glendarroch. Old pallets removed from Craichlaw now proving useful. I would prefer to have stone or flagged pegs but I can't afford such luxuries.*
> *Two platforms are built and nailed into position, six more swims identified. In total there are now nine swims 'fishable'. It really is back-breaking work.*
> *A few brief fishing sessions have produced only perch and rudd so far. The water is crystal clear and very shallow, 5 ft deep max. Think I'll invest in some Canal Black.*

Glendarroch Loch; Bream.

Both of these waters were very susceptible to temperature fluctuation. Being so shallow they warmed up quickly, but equally, a cool night or a Northerly wind could kill the fishing stone dead.

Craichlaw Loch gave a glimpse of its potential when a period of warm May weather saw anglers catch tench to 3.5lb and in good numbers. Fishing into dawn then an hour into daylight, or at dusk and an hour into darkness, would invariably produce double-figure bags of hard-fighting tench. Meanwhile the large carp continued to elude capture, invariably smashing up anglers who fished on lighter tackle for tench but declining any bait offered by carp anglers on sturdier terminal tackle.

The presence of so many lilies was of great benefit to the carp in particular. If you could finally tempt them to take the bait, they would scream off on powerful runs directly into the dense beds of thick lilies. The small carp I'd stocked a month ago showed up well, though, with reports of seven or eight carp at a sitting, all taken on floating pellet (I wondered why – what could they possibly have been fed on in their stock ponds?)

Light, pre-baiting around the margins and edges of the lilies often improved the chances of success, but only particles or loose feed, heavy ground-baiting had the opposite effect.

Typical Craichlaw tench of 3lb 2oz. Summer 1992.

Glendarroch Loch also continued to improve as the weeks went by, with some quality rudd and roach coming out. Some of the rudd were real quality specimens of anything between 1lb and 2lb! Superbly coloured, with a russet/crimson/golden hue, they were hard to catch, requiring light tackle to tempt a bite, but providing a vigorous and hard-fought battle to land successfully. The real surprise came when Kev and I caught Crucian carp, a bonus species that must have survived the draining as I hadn't stocked them.

Snake Escape . . .

I received a further surprise one evening, when I hit into a huge eel. It was by far and away the largest eel I have ever witnessed, never mind caught. I played it for a good twenty minutes before finally, and with great relief, sliding the landing net under it. I must confess to being slightly daunted at the prospect of unhooking it, as it wriggled and writhed with great energy and obvious displeasure. To this day I'm not quite sure where I went wrong, but as I took the hook out using my forceps it gave a mighty twist and slithered out of the net, down the bank and into the water, leaving me stunned and bitterly disappointed not being able to either photograph or weigh the anaconda-type beast. At a conservative estimate I would say that eel was somewhere between 4lb and 5lb in weight.

Reflections

As we headed into early summer, and with our first full year complete, it was time to reflect, learn and plan for the future.

The guest house was becoming increasingly busy. The May Bank Holidays and the Easter break brought more trade, and our policy of investing in advertising seemed to be paying off. But we could not afford another bleak winter like the last one. We now understood just how much money we needed to make during spring through to autumn to ensure business survival during the austere winter months.

I was also aware of just how much more I needed to offer guests, including the shooting fraternity and visiting anglers, by way of sporting options.

The forward business plan was:
   i)   To seek lease deals for other coarse fishing waters.
   ii)   To seek access to trout and salmon fishing.
   iii)   To develop sea-fishing opportunities.
   iv)   To explore how best to provide coarse angler's tackle and bait.
   v)   To advertise in the shooting and wildfowling press.

vi) To liaise with the local tourist board regarding the golf and cycling market.

The guest house needed constant upgrading, from the décor to the kitchen equipment and guest facilities (such as a drying room). We had the top floor open for accommodation now, and we desperately needed another shower and toilet facility on that floor. Could we afford it? We needed to speak, yet again, to our now not-quite-so-friendly bank manager.

At the same time, as a family we needed to ensure that we spent as much time as possible with our children and not become utterly distracted by the demands of the business at the expense of our kids. It was to be a tricky exercise in plate-spinning.

We spent some of the fishery income on an advertising campaign that included T-shirts and adhesive tackle box logos. When deciding on clothing sizes I looked at my own physique and that of most visiting anglers and ordered just a few items of Small and Medium sized clothing, and rather more Large and XXL.

Jackie and author Ken. Seen at the front door of The Palakona Guest House, Ken is modelling the latest in fashionable fishery business apparel of 1992.

Yet Another Water

One of the waters the previous owner had claimed to have fishing rights for but didn't, was a very small but wonderfully located farm pond of about two thirds of an acre, called Culscadden Farm Pond. I had fished it in previous years, catching tench, roach, rudd, perch and very rarely, carp.

Culscadden Farm Pond.

The attraction of the pond to me was its location, being just a hundred yards or so from a shingle beach by the sea. This factor alone had business value as a clear marketing attraction – a fishing spot likely to appeal to families. Dad could fish, while Mum sunbathed on the beach, or perhaps both played with the kids during picnic breaks from the fishing, just walking distance away. As a bonus it also gave access to some wonderful sea fishing marks. A deal was soon struck with the amiable owner Tom Simpson, a local farmer.

I was delighted to have the fishing rights but, just as with Glendarroch Loch, the venue needed much work before I could sell any day tickets. There were no pegs, platforms or hard standing. Bushes impeded access to one bank, while the other was prone to muddy, boggy, car-traps in wet weather.

There were a couple of remote but beautifully located cottages next to the pond and I feared the residents would object to too many visiting anglers and their vehicles. One of these residents was our local traffic-warden; I certainly didn't want to upset him.

I went to the trouble of speaking to the inhabitants of all the nearby homes. They seemed less concerned than I did, pointing out that they were used to the many sea anglers that came to visit anyway. Nevertheless, I decided to limit the numbers of day tickets to be sold on any one day.

It was fortunate that much of the work on Glendarroch Loch was nearing completion because this new water proved to be more time-consuming to make fishable than I'd anticipated. God bless Kev, he came to help me out whenever he could, but of course he was working full-time now, so much of the work fell to me and my increasingly aching back.

The roadside bushes were hacked back and pegs fashioned, a bog-free car-parking area identified and cleared. Pegs and swims were gradually formed on the far side. But the most time-consuming and taxing job was the weed clearance. The pond was deceptive to the eye, appearing to be largely weed free; indeed there very few lilies or other emergent aquatic plants. But hidden under the surface . . . aaghhh! The dreaded Hornwort and Canadian Pondweed were flourishing, and in vast quantities.

The local fisheries officer suggested that the reason for the incredible weed growth was probably the frequent use of fertilisers and nitrates used on the adjacent fields. These fields drained directly into the pond, as did a small burn via a natural spring. Just as the fertilisers boosted the yield of the farm produce, so it had the same effect on the weeds.

It took me hour upon hour of hard labour to even make a dent in the dreaded green stuff. In one particular spot I had lifted so much weed out of the water that I had no more space left on the bank to pile it up and had to use a wheelbarrow to clear the damn stuff away.

A Startling Discovery

I continued working away at Culscadden Pond, often in the evenings, when time away from bailiffing duties at Craichlaw and Glendarroch, and helping Jackie at the guest house would permit. On one such evening I was working alone on the far bank, where the water was shallow, but then suddenly fell away to approximately six ft deep. It was getting late and the light was beginning to fade.

I was clearing the weeds using a double-headed rake on a sturdy rope when, as I retrieved the rake, it became entangled in something fairly heavy, moving below. I pulled harder. Whatever it was gradually began to come towards me. To my utter horror, a hand and then an arm broke the surface beyond.

I was tempted to just drop everything and run for help, but I also felt I owed it to whomever it was that had met such a sad end to persevere, and to retrieve their remains with due deference and without delay. With a few more tentative tugs on the rope the body appeared.

The evening gloom was setting in, and the body was some way out; it was difficult to make out much detail. Was it young or old, male or female? I couldn't tell, as the body and head were covered in weed and slime. I just wanted to bring the remains to the side where I could secure it before going to seek help.

I'd loosened my grip on the rope in the panic, but despite this the corpse was free from its sub-aquatic chains and remained floating on the surface, slowly turning on itself in a gruesome parody of a giddy snorkel diver. I cautiously waded in deeper, getting closer until I was able to make out more details. The body was naked, its limbs pink and strangely shiny. The head was completely bald, and its feet were bent at complete right-angles.

With a mixture of huge relief, accompanied by a sense of foolishness and anger, I suddenly realised what I was dealing with. My 'body' was a mannequin – a shop dummy! I dragged it in closer, no longer concerned with showing this 'person' any respect, and threw it on the bank-side, venting my anger at the unknown idiot who thought that doing this was a funny prank, a good laugh. If I could've got my hands on the person responsible at that moment, there would have been a real body in the water!

I made enquiries the following day, and discovered that my anger was partly misplaced. Apparently, the dummy had been erected by the previous trout fishing syndicate as a scarecrow to frighten away cormorants, herons and otters. Over time it had fallen into the water where it had been forgotten, until my rake disturbed it from its watery grave.

Evening at Culscadden Farm Pond, the location of the dead 'body'.

Summer Days . . .

Diary Entry, June/July 1992:
Stunning bags of tench from Craichlaw. Stan Watson had weights of 62lb one morning from one of the driveway swims, the largest being 6lb 2oz. In fact over the three days he was our guest he landed over 100lb of tench. I fished his swim the following day and blanked!
Tench spawning in the middle of a sustained heat-wave, fascinating observing them close up. They are so preoccupied that I swear I could wade in and pick them up!
carp lads from Glasgow could only catch tench on strawberry flavoured boilies. They did observe up to a dozen carp basking or cruising on the surface but no takes off the top.
Tony watched a large carp cruise under the bridge, estimated the weight to be 15lb-17lb and with 7-8 large scales down its back.

The Story of 'Daffy', Our Pet Duck

One morning, I noticed a kerfuffle going on at the bottom of what was a very long garden. The previous owner had installed small, shallow breeding ponds in the lawn, and something was splashing around in one of them. Our cat, Misty, was still with us at the time this story is set and I could see him trying to catch something. It was only as I approached that I could make out a very small duckling, one short of quite a few feathers too. He'd had a lucky escape by the look of him, bedraggled, terrified and with nowhere to hide.

I assumed that he had become separated from his family or they hadn't survived the sometime cruelty of Mother Nature and had fled the river that ran near the bottom of the garden, seeking refuge in the nearest piece of water he could find, even if this was just a shallow tray of rainwater!

I chased away the loitering cat and set about constructing a shelter for the poor wee thing. It's amazing what you can achieve with a roll of chicken wire and some battens, necessity being the mother of invention.

My two daughters soon adopted him as another family pet, naming him Daffy and checked up on his well-being before and after school. He was well fed, preferring sweetcorn, but accepting almost anything including small worms, tadpoles and various pond weeds. He positively thrived, meaning I had to keep extending his safety-pen to include higher and wider caging as he grew from an ugly duckling into a beautifully coloured Mallard drake.

After a few months, particularly when he started to try to fly, it was clear that my DIY skills did not extend to building an aviary, and it became obvious he would need to be returned to the wild.

The girls were surprisingly fine about this, and I decided Glendarroch Loch would be as safe a place as any to release him. There had been an existing group of wild ducks in residence there, and I thought he would just have to take his chances at being accepted by them.

Daffy wasn't too pleased with the transfer process! He didn't like being trapped in a pike landing net and then transferred in a cage; the poor lad found it all quite traumatic judging by just how quickly he flew away as soon as I let him out by the waterside.

I needn't have feared for his welfare. Whenever I visited the loch, which I did almost daily during the summer months given my bailiffing duties, he was always there. I had to explain to anglers what was going on as I shouted "Daffy, oh Daffy," before a duck would appear to take sweetcorn fed by hand!

I doubted that he would survive the shooting season as autumn arrived, but somehow he got through it and over-wintered successfully. He gradually became less willing to respond to my calls, until he eventually blended into his surroundings altogether and I couldn't tell him apart from all the other drakes on the loch.

I like to think that his progeny exist within the current group of ducks that reside within the loch's parameters all these years later, and occasionally, though strictly only when alone, I shout out his name, just in case. No reply as yet.

Life Outside the Bubble

Learning to run a multi-stream business, excuse the pun, with no previous experience whatsoever, was proving very difficult and time-consuming. We had made this move to try to improve our lifestyle and to redress our work-life balance, yet it was having quite the opposite effect.

Jackie was kept very busy running the accommodation side of things. The nearest wholesaler was in Stranraer, a 50-mile round trip away, and given that we often never knew until late at night how many people wanted breakfast or evening meals the logistics of food storage and preparation were difficult. Every morning beds had to be made, sheets changed, rooms cleaned. Packed lunches were to be prepared, evening meals readied and cooked.

Meanwhile, I was busy clearing swims, exploring new waters, experimenting with baits and techniques. I also needed to be on hand for our guests, driving and/or guiding them to various fishing venues, issuing day tickets, and bailiffing the various waters. I helped with serving meals in the guest house, and when we'd had a large group check-out, cleaning the rooms and lifting laundry.

We had parental commitments on top of all this, too. Our two daughters were everything in our lives, and we'd made this move partly in the hope of improving their prospects. We had to find time for them. Fortunately they had both settled into their respective schools, where they were performing well, and had made many new friends. They enjoyed overnight sleepovers, trips to the local beaches, burns, forests and shops. We tried to find time to do all the 'family' activities. Having doting Grandparents nearby helped too, of course!

Despite being so busy at home, it was important to look up over the turret at life out in the wider world. Of course we watched the news, but it didn't seem to have the same relevance to us as it used to. Much of it was very depressing anyway. The UK was in an ever-deepening economic depression, and John Major had won a surprise General Election victory for the Tories despite this, arguably helped by the *Sun* newspaper running an 'anti-Kinnock' campaign.

IRA bombs were exploding with deadly effect all over the UK. The sectarian violence claimed its 3,000[th] victim.

Coal mines and steelworks were closing, while towns and cities across the UK experienced riots as the effects of rising unemployment took their toll.

AIDS was increasing across the world.

It was a year that the Queen would later describe as her "Annus Horribilis".

And yet, this was the very time that we had decided to open a business that relied to a large extent on northern, working class males for custom! What were we thinking of?

With the benefit of hindsight, it was arguably a good time to aim at the fishing and activity holiday market. Holidays abroad were beyond the financial means of many families, who were facing uncertain times as the recession bit deeper. 'Staycations', as they later became known, or weekend breaks, were often the only kind of holiday many families could afford.

Here in Newton Stewart in 1992, the busiest places in town were undoubtedly the Job Centre and benefits office. Elsewhere in the neighbourhood, John Major made a 'goodwill visit', to open the new Health Centre, and Stenna launched their 'SeaCat' ferry service, promising journey times from Stranraer to Belfast in an impressive 90 minutes.

Meanwhile, the headline in the local newspaper, the *Galloway Gazette*, lamented 'Job losses, liquidations and company closures.'

Probably best to stay in our bubble, after all . . .

6 THE SEASONS TURN . . .

As the summer of 1992 turned to autumn, work on the lochs and accommodation continued unabated. Day-tickets continued to sell well for all our three waters, while I had also negotiated a deal to sell day-tickets for the local Forestry Commission waters.

We gradually improved the guest house facilities with new TVs in the rooms, new beds and carpeting, and a slow but steady programme of other cost-limited improvements.

I was busy working hard at Craichlaw Loch one day when Derek the gardener informed me that Andrew Gladstone had become engaged. This was joyous, if somewhat unexpected news. 'Degs' told me her name was Mary, and that at that very moment she was out at the other side of the loch, painting the bridge. It was encouraging to hear that she was 'getting stuck-in' along with the rest of us, and I felt obliged to go and introduce myself. I rounded the bend on the far side of the loch, and sure enough, there was a young lady painting the bridge. She had a palette, watercolours, an easel and brush in hand.

To be fair, Mary was a well-qualified landscape designer, and put all her skills to good use; Craichlaw House and its surroundings were transformed over the next few years.

Scuba divers . . .

An unexpected bonus appeared one weekend, when a group of Scuba divers booked into the guest house. They had arranged to dive in Wigtown Bay, and came back from their first outing with a box full of lobsters. Jackie was away that weekend, and I had to cook the crustaceans. Never again! I'd heard about how they squealed as they were dropped into the boiling pot, but hadn't experienced it personally until I had to handle these poor things. I couldn't sleep that night.

Despite this, I enjoyed chatting to the divers. Diving was a pursuit I had always wanted to try (and eventually did, many years later.) They explained how they often also dived in lakes and quarries near their home town of Morecambe. Not one to miss an opportunity, I asked them to consider exploring Craichlaw Loch to see if they could locate the mythical deep hole that the previous owner claimed existed out in the middle.

Poor weather at sea prevented them from sea-diving on the last day of their stay, so they offered to dive Craichlaw instead. I watched, fascinated and envious in equal measure, contemplating what it must be like to be underwater with carp and bream and tench on their terms and in their own environment.

Divers exploring Craichlaw Loch

The divers weren't under water for too long, having found the visibility (viz) somewhat limited. It proved only too easy to make this viz even worse by unintentionally stirring up the silty bottom with their fins. They were able to confirm that there was a constant depth in the deeper areas of the loch of seven to eight feet, but that no deep hole existed. They did see various species of fish, but as they weren't anglers they could only recognise carp and shoals of perch. The carp were invariably sluggish to move, but would then surge away with power and speed after being disturbed.

As I watched the proceedings with the divers' designated bank-side safety-officer alongside me, large carp could be seen cruising through the very areas that the divers had just vacated. Were they inquisitive, or feeding through the stirred-up silt? Perhaps both.

A Fishing Legend Comes to Stay . . .

Graham Marsden is a well-known figure in the world of coarse fishing, best known for his incredible record of bream, barbel and pike catches but also for writing various highly successful and entertaining angling books.

I couldn't quite believe it when he agreed to fish Craichlaw Loch with his father-in-law while he was paying a visit to the area. Once I overcame my tongue-tied, awe-struck shyness, Graham proved to be affable, friendly and very helpful.

Diary Entry, September 1992:
Bream expert Graham Marsden fished peg 16 at Craichlaw today. He bagged up with good quality roach but no bream as hoped. He believes that any bream present are few in number and probably small in size. Graham insists that tench, carp and bream do not mix well being competitive feeders. He suggests that I consider exchanging roach of which I have many, for bream, of which I have few but to keep carp and tench stocks in separate waters.
He very kindly sent me a 'Cobra' groundbait throwing stick, excellent it is too!
Also... Tony Taylor caught another small carp from the holding pond and transferred it into Glendarroch Loch.

Total of stock transferred into Glendarroch since I took over now stands at . . .
Tench x 10, and Carp x 11.

Farewell to Clare . . . Hello to Digger

Our much-loved family pet dog, Clare, had been a substitute child for Jackie and me when we first got together back in 1976. We rescued her as a puppy from the cat and dog shelter in Claremont Road, Newcastle-upon-Tyne, hence her name. A 'Heinz 57' mongrel, Clare was wonderfully placid. She'd been there through our various house moves, the arrival of our children, and she'd even had a litter of her own. While out on walks she would listen to every problem I shared without judging me. She tolerated our kids pulling her whiskers and climbing on her back when they were young. In short, Clare was one of the family in every way.

She was 14 years old when we moved, and we knew she wouldn't have long left. She adapted well to the change of environment initially, though, enjoying short walks along the river and exploring the enormous garden.

Eventually, however, she couldn't face life any longer. She was virtually blind, became incontinent, disoriented and almost immobile. One morning we found her standing in the kitchen, staring at the wall shaking and completely unresponsive to our calls. Various visits to the local vet had prepared us for what was likely to come next, and that morning we realised that the time had come. We took her to the vet for the final time, and she slipped away as gently as she had lived her life. Jackie was preparing soup that evening; it was much saltier than usual.

I buried Clare beneath the apple tree in the garden and swore I'd never have another dog.

Digger

My 'dog-free' resolve only lasted a few months! I missed the company, loyalty and friendship that only a dog can provide. Before long we made the trip to the dog rescue centre at nearby Dunragit, where a lively, bouncing wee puppy chose us to be his family.

From the moment he got in the car he was an absolute bundle of energy. We nearly lost him on the way home, when he attempted to leap out of the car window with puppy exuberance as I drove at 60mph.

He proved to be a real character in every 'doggy' way – friendly, energetic, nosy and loyal. He earned his name by constantly digging up Jackie's bedding plants in the back yard. The name was sealed when a visiting pike angler pointed out he had a dog with the name. It just seemed to fit.

Digger proved popular with the guests, as small puppies invariably are. He was generous in every way. One morning Jackie and I were in the kitchen when one of two trout anglers came in carrying their breakfast plates. "That was lovely, Jackie," he said, in a strong Liverpool accent, "but we couldn't manage the two extra sausages little Digger left us!" I knew instantly what he meant. Digger, not yet fully house trained, had deposited two 'sausages' at their feet beneath the table. Naughty Digger!

As he grew, Digger became my second in command as I went about my various fishery duties. Sometimes he'd notice me putting on my coat or work-boots and I'd find him in the car waiting for me. He loved water, and enjoyed nothing more than splashing around in river, loch or sea.

As Digger matured, he became a little more obedient and controllable, but appearances can be deceptive. One morning, I went for a bailiff check-up at Craichlaw Loch with my ever-faithful hound accompanying me. It was very early and quiet, with only one car in the car park when we arrived. Digger and I enjoyed a walk around the loch, looking at the fizzing bubbles of tench on the feed, and the carp crashing and splashing amongst the lily pads.

We went over the bridge to the island where we came across a carp angler who gestured to me to keep low and be quiet. As we both bent down out of the skyline, he pointed to a number of carp feeding on the surface, one of which was particularly large. He explained in whispers that he'd been here since before dawn, having made the two-hour journey down from Glasgow. He had been slowly enticing the carp into his swim to feed, with free offerings of floating boilies, pellets and bread-crust, but with no luck yet. He further explained that of course he fully intended to come for a day-ticket later in the day.

The angler crept forward slowly to the edge of the loch, and cast in with a large piece of bread-crust on a greased floating line. At this point Digger just couldn't control himself. He saw the bread in the air and leapt after it, landing in the water with a huge splash that created a tidal wave of disturbance.

The carp all vanished, never to be seen again that morning. Digger returned to the bank, shaking himself dry all over the angler and his carefully laid out tackle, while clearly hoping the angler would throw more bread in. This was a great game! I made my apologies and left. Naughty Digger, again.

The angler packed up his gear in a huff and headed back from whence he'd came. He never did call in to pay for his day-ticket.

Digger swim-jumping in typical fashion.

Shooters Missing

Late autumn 1992 was cold and wet, with the local fishing scene quiet. Having spent hard-earned money on advertising in the *Shooting Times*, we were hoping that the shooting fraternity, wildfowlers, deer stalkers and rough shooters would begin to make their plans and start booking in. We were sadly disappointed! We had so much to learn about these particular guests.

One chap who helped me understand field sports better was Percy Betts. Percy was a wise old cockney owl with his own inland wildfowling business. He lived just across the road from Craichlaw, and always welcomed a visitor for a cup of coffee, or something stronger.

When we first moved into the area I was warned by more than one of the locals that if I'd shaken hands with Percy Betts I should count my fingers. But to be fair I never had any major problems with him. I sent him inland wildfowling trade, we benefited from the accommodation trade they provided, and as a bonus Percy educated me on their ways.

One thing I learnt quickly from Percy was to follow the cues of nature. The geese would arrive when nature told them to, and not before. This advice was true for the salmon anglers, too – the local spate rivers would only fish well after spells of rain. This led to late bookings amongst one of the few groups of visitors who eagerly awaited rain in the weather forecast! The weather, far more than set legal shooting-season dates, would dictate when wildfowling, deer-stalking or rough shooting would or would not proceed. The distinction between 'could' and 'would' was a life lesson for me, as well. Booking accommodation months ahead was not something the wildfowlers in particular could afford to do, in case their quarry hadn't arrived.

Like them, we just had to wait . . .

Experiments from Hawaii (Honestly!)

One morning, I heard from a visitor from Hawaii, named Knud Lindgren. He was staying at a nearby guest house, but was very keen to speak to me about local coarse fishing and called around for a chat.

It transpired that Knud was a fishery biologist, who had spent a number of years developing a 'magic formula' fish bait. This I had to see. It came in a paste, or as thin, brown-coloured sticks that became pliable in water. Knud told me that this special bait contained various natural chemicals that acted as both appetite stimulants and flavour attractants, triggering fish feeding.

I explained that the water temperature was low, it being a Scottish

November, and that most of the carp and tench were not feeding freely. Knud was still confident of success, and insisted that we at least experiment.

I went to Craichlaw Loch, fishing off various pegs and at various depths, but with only limited success. The magic formula certainly seemed to attract perch, roach and brown trout, of which I caught many. But of course without another angler fishing the same place using maggot or worm to compare the magic bait against, no real conclusions could be reached. Indeed as a scientifically valid experiment, the variables, controls, methods and measures were all open to criticism.

Knud was not disappointed, however, telling me that he was certain the water temperature was the key factor in triggering the chemical reactions and that as a result, our experiment was of real value to him. He did send me some more of his concoctions the following summer for me to use in warmer water temperatures. I even used it in subsequent years in Cyprus, but I'm afraid I have to report that they were no more successful than traditional baits.

Diary entry, November 1992
STOCKING!
I'm sure most anglers enjoy stockings but I have never, ever enjoyed such pleasure as was afforded by these particular stockings.
Everything went like clockwork. I met Don Patterson from the Barony College, Dumfries at The Little Chef car-park at 7:00 a.m. where I joined him in his pick-up and transportation tank. Don needed some carp for his fisheries department so we agreed to share the transportation costs. We travelled to Killington Lake Service Station off the M6 where at mid-morning the carp supplier, William Banks, all the way from Worcestershire, arrived with our fish.
The transfer went well. All the fish look healthy and powerful. Don wasn't sure that all the 8 x 2lb carp he

had ordered were present but with time pressing we could not afford to hang around. The journey back was uneventful with just a couple of quick check up stops needed to reassure us of the health of the fish.

We arrived at Craichlaw Loch at 4:00 p.m. and, in the midst of a heavy hailstorm and having ensured gradual equal water temperatures, introduced the carp into both Craichlaw and Glendarroch in almost darkness. Don's concerns were unfounded, all his 2lb fish were present and correct. What was also clear was that there were far more ghost carp present than I'd expected particularly in the 1lb-2lb range, 54 in total. The 250 crucian carp were all in good order too.

I am delighted with the mirrors and commons, most are around the 5lb-6lb mark but one weighed in at 7lb-2oz! Beautifully marked and in great condition with no netting marks, ulcers or lip wounds. As promised these are fresh fish, carp never previously fished for.

Craichlaw Loch now holds approximately 130 carp of varying weights and 200 Crucians around the 10-12 oz mark. Glendarroch now has a population of 70 carp all around the 2lb mark. I'm pleased with the spread of size and type but I do worry about the vulnerability of the ghosties having seen their beautiful markings.

Glendarroch Loch, November 1992.

I kept a watchful eye for fatalities over the following weeks, but only a few occurred. My concerns for the beautifully marked Ghost carp were proven justified when one of about 2lb-3lb was found floating and barely alive in the margins. It had clear slash marks to either side of its body, almost certainly caused by the beak of the ever-present cormorant or heron.

I brought the Ghost carp home and treated it with all medical care in my fish ICU. It made some progress, and I was able to transfer it to the local commercial aquarium at Skyreburn, run by my pal Neil Parkes. Fast forward a few weeks, and just as it seemed to be recovering well, it sadly and inexplicably died. I'm pleased to report that it didn't live up to its species name and come back to haunt either of us.

Winter 92/93

November and December saw cold and frosty weather dominate the world of The Palakona Guest House and Craichlaw Fisheries. This meant only limited passing trade, but gradually increasing numbers of inland wildfowlers.

While work on the various fisheries continued outside in the bracing Scottish air, at home it was time again to reflect and to plan ahead.

The plan for 1993 and beyond was really just a continuation of the previous years, namely, to develop the fishery business while improving the existing accommodation. We also hoped to broaden the target group of activity-focused visitors.

We had to invest what little savings we had managed to scrape together, on the established basis of having to 'speculate to accumulate'. Improving the guests' experience was crucial for our reputation, both via word of mouth and also to meet increasingly stringent Tourist Board standards of accommodation.

We installed log-burning stoves in both lounges, and opened up the coal fire in the larger guest lounge. Jackie set-to decorating the bedrooms, making the difficult decisions about what decor would appeal to the wide range of customers we attracted. The anglers and shooters didn't want floral paper and pink paintwork, but the families and passing ferry trade customers didn't want magnolia and camouflage green! Somehow Jackie managed a compromise which, judging from the positive comments in our Visitors Book, suited everyone.

I tried to find sufficient money in the accounts to consider another fish stocking. The price of carp was exorbitant, in my view at least! Carp over 4lb would cost at least £4 per pound. The prices escalated proportionately, up to an amazing £250 for a 20lb fish! This was well out of my price range, so my plan was to buy at lower weights and bring them on.

An Interesting Christmas

As Christmas approached, we counted our pennies carefully. Times were tight across the UK in a terrible recession, and we were no different. We provided flexible accommodation and meals for a company building concrete farm buildings nearby for a couple of months. They were a pleasant, jovial bunch of lads from Leeds who put in long hours, often working into the dark. This meant late evening meals for Jackie to prepare and me to serve.

The leader of this group mentioned that he was selling his Amstrad computer with various games included. My two daughters were desperate for exactly such a thing for Christmas, and a deal was soon struck. It was our first ever computer, and what fun we had, working out how to set it up and then how to install and play the games – the former taking much longer than the latter. Looking back it was all so primitive, but at the time it was wonderful!

We had decided that Christmas Day and Boxing Day would be the only two days of the year we would be closed. This was family time; time for our kids and for us.

We bade the last of our guests farewell. The 'No Vacancies' sign was put on prominent display, the always open front stable-type door was firmly closed, and the illuminated sign switched off.

We attended the outdoor Carol singing at Dashwood Square in the town, and came home settling in to watch the usual Christmas Fare on TV, including *Santa Claus: The Movie* followed by the *Paul Daniels Christmas Magic Show*, while ITV thrilled us with *Emmerdale* and *The Bill*. (I knew I should've gone fishing.)

A quiet family evening ensued, until the doorbell rang. I initially thought it would be friends calling in to wish us a Happy Christmas, and to arrange to drag me out to The Black Horse later, firmly against my wishes and not at all previously arranged . . . But no, I was confronted by two young women with suitcases and a forlorn look on their faces. It soon became apparent that they came from Belgium.

Neither could speak fluent English, and I wasn't even sure what language was spoken in Belgium. However, my mastery of the French language, learnt at school and delivered in a Wigan accent, came to the rescue. Well, sort of. Phonetically, it sounded something like:

"Bonjewer madams, cummontaleyvoo?"

When combined with sign language, we managed enough between the three of us to establish their story. It transpired that they had come off the last ferry from Ireland before the Christmas shut-down and, not having pre-arranged forward public transport or accommodation, found themselves stranded in little old Newton Stewart. Apparently, they simply hadn't realised the entire UK virtually closed down for Christmas. What made matters even more complicated for them was that they were students back-packing around Europe with very limited money until the UK banks re-opened. This was a Thursday, and no banks would be open until Monday. They opened their purses and offered me all they had, which amounted to a paltry few pounds plus loose change. At that time we charged £13 per person per night, and they were a few bob short to say the least. Tears began to flow.

A quick visual check suggested neither of them was pregnant. Neither was there a donkey in sight. I looked to the skies for a bright star in the East, but I couldn't see one, not even with my binoculars, (well you can't be too careful in such circumstances). I reminded myself that we did have a stable in the out-house.

I was faced with a dilemma; this poor pair of weary travellers had already tried other hotels and guest houses in town, and had either been turned away or found them to be far too expensive. We were possibly their last hope before a sleeping-bag in the nearby bus-shelter beckoned. Yet Jackie and I had promised ourselves and our family that we would have a guest-free Christmas. What was I to do?

I invited the two girls in out of the cold and asked them to wait while I went to explain this moral dilemma to the family. The kids didn't mind at all, quite rightly failing to see how it might affect them. Jackie and I didn't debate it for long either; we really couldn't do anything other than to offer them a room. I did explain to the ladies that while we could offer them breakfast it would be more of a 'brunch' and that we weren't doing any evening meals until the 27th. They were more than happy with this arrangement.

We enjoyed a pleasant, quiet, family Christmas. Of course we invited our two guests to join us for Christmas dinner, and again on Boxing Day. In the evenings we asked them to join us for a few festive drinks, but they politely declined all such offers, presumably not wishing to be an imposition. Indeed they were so quiet we barely knew they were there. Occasionally I would see them coming or going, they seemed to enjoy walking in the local hills.

On the morning that they left, they discovered that the London bus out of town would depart before the banks would open and that the cash-machines were all empty. I asked them how much their bus fare was, and left them with sufficient funds to purchase their tickets, taking a nominal amount out of what was left for their three-night stay. This came to the sum total of not very much at all.

Well, it was Christmas . . .

Back to Business for 1993

Meanwhile the seasons turned, as ever. The geese had arrived in increasing numbers just before Christmas on the foreshore of

Wigtown Bay, and the wildfowlers were soon to follow, taking over from the inland wildfowlers whose season ended on January 31st.

Our extensive advertising and marketing campaign, coupled with word of mouth, seemed to be working as accommodation numbers increased markedly. We had shooters from across the UK and sometimes Europe too. Sporting groups from Holland, Germany and even Italy came to stay, bringing their unique ways with them.

One large group of Italian rough-shooters re-arranged the entire dining-room into one large table setting. They then set about pooling all the food, which we served as individual meals, into large bowls and sharing it all out as a communal 'all you can eat' type of buffet. They then added large amounts of bread, parmesan cheese and gallons of wine that they'd brought with them to the feast. An Italian-style evening meal lasted for two hours and was a loud, fun-filled and lively affair.

This group of fifteen loud, emotional and very friendly Italians only had one person amongst them who could speak English to translate for us. Mealtimes were such fun whenever he wasn't present, and he did so enjoy the conviviality offered by the pubs of Newton Stewart that his absences were frequent and lengthy. Working out what 'Mayonnaise' translated as in Italian was a particular challenge.

One of this group expressed real interest in shooting a Haggis. Before setting out on this trip his daughter, who just happened to be studying the poetry of Robert Burns at college in Italy, had pleaded with her father to at the very least take a photograph of a Haggis in the wild even if he couldn't manage to actually shoot one. Our Italian visitor fell for this wind-up completely. His friends kept it alive throughout the week. I promised him through the translator that if he did get a sizeable Haggis then Jackie would prepare it for the evening meal.

The Gamekeeper who had taken the lads out all week was also in on the ruse, but took me to one side on the final day to inform me that he had been harangued and confronted by this one chap berating him bitterly for not leading them to any Haggis! Apparently, he intended to write and complain to anyone and everyone he could think of.

The final moments of their stay involved me taking a group photograph of them all, during which the translator broke the news, in a very loud voice, that Haggis were a mythological beast and that our friend had been well and truly 'had!' The group literally fell about, falling on the floor in a typically effusive Italian manner and howling with laughter as tears rolled down their cheeks. The victim also took it all in good stead coming over to shake my hand and embrace me. I never did see the promised copy of those photographs, wish I had.

Troubleshooting?

Not all shooting trips ended quite so amicably. I came downstairs one morning having heard a ruckus in the hall. About five guests were standing in the hallway, with a couple of suitcases and various bits of shooting equipment lying by the front door. One of the group was stood nursing a bloodied nose, while his son was cursing and swearing, threatening anyone and everyone. The group leader told me to keep out of it, and that things would be sorted. I did as I was told, and hid in the kitchen (this is called discretion, not cowardice).

Some time later the full details of the incident were revealed. The shooters were from a club in Yorkshire, and had been out that morning wildfowling. The chap with the bloodied nose and his adult son were isolated hill farmers, and weren't well known to the rest of the group. Apparently, his dog was faithful and loyal but getting very old. It was slow to retrieve, and found rough terrain hard to negotiate, slowing the owners down. The poor animal would be heard whimpering after strenuous exercise, and was partially deaf.

That morning the owner and son shot various geese, but the dog had been unable to locate and thus retrieve any of them. As the shoot ended and the group started to gather in readiness to return to the guest house, the loud report of a shot being fired was heard from amidst nearby bushes.

The hill farmer had shot his dog and hurled the corpse into the nearest culvert for the tide to take out. He defended his actions, claiming he had done the right thing, and that it was only right and proper that he should end the poor dog's suffering quickly. In his opinion, it had been an act of mercy. He claimed that such practice was commonplace amongst the hill farming fraternity.

However, this heartless act caused great anger amongst the group. A fight had broken out, leading to the guilty person and his son being ordered to leave their company forthwith. They were physically thrown out of the front door of the guest house. Their luggage landed on the pavement behind them, and they were told to find their own way home.

Some weeks later the same club returned. They informed me that the guilty party had been thrown out the club and banned sine die. I was out one night having a few beers with them, when the incident came up in conversation. I asked why it was considered such a huge crime of dishonour to shoot a dog, but not so a goose, deer, a fox or pheasant? It was a short-lived conversation.

A Generous Tip?

On another occasion, a pair of Dutch wildfowlers kindly left their entire bag of 12 geese behind. They didn't tell us about it in advance – they just left the birds hanging in the garage when they departed one morning! Thankfully Kev, now working in the local butchers, knew how to make good use of them. He sold some, froze some and ate some. He was sprouting feathers by the time he'd finished them off.

A 'kind donation' of geese left behind.

Ponds in Hiding

I finally located the series of small ponds hidden away in the bushes near Glendarroch Loch, of which I'd heard plenty. These had been excavated by a previous fish farming entrepreneur a few years ago, who'd been hoping to make his fortune by breeding carp in rural Scotland. What could possibly go wrong?

The ponds were approximately six yards square and perhaps three feet deep, with a water supply coming from the nearby burn. They did appeal to me as having some potential as temporary holding ponds, in which I could develop young carp until they were big enough to be stocked into their home water. The growth rate of carp is phenomenal if fed well, and the holding pond idea gave me food for thought.

Meanwhile the pike anglers, both local and visitors were beginning to enjoy themselves . . .

Diary Entries, February/March 1993:
Very mild spell continues. Two lads from Ipswich had an enjoyable day on the river Bladnoch taking 13 pike, best of 7lb-4oz. They blanked on Maberry but then had a busy session on The White Loch (Monreith) where they took 11 pike to 8lb-11oz. They reported many male pike in Boat House Bay; queens will be due to join them any day now.
Kev and I fished Craichlaw in the dark one evening. We caught one roach and one trout!
Oh yes, I seem to have negotiated a deal for 250 small Mirror carp @ 50p each plus 4 large Ghost carp at 16lb each (£260!) Just a matter of finding the money and then sorting out the bream order!
Cutting trees at Craichlaw was hard and sweaty work, just how Kev or I didn't fall in I don't know! We found a dead Tench of about 3lb in the weir. Suspicious slash marks on its back, almost certainly that bloody

> *cormorant again.*
> *With temperatures rising Kev and I fished Glendarroch*
> *this afternoon. I had 53 fish, perch and rudd, poor*
> *Kev blanked!*

Easter, and another exciting development

I was asked to develop the coarse fishing facilities at a local caravan park that was keen to broaden its appeal to holiday makers. I noted the deal in my diary as ' . . . *lease of £250 p.a. for three years plus I keep 50% of all day tickets sold. They will pay start-up costs, stocking, maintenance and advertising. I will create swims, and access path, fishing platforms and provide consultancy and expertise.*' I formalised it into a typed lease agreement, and left it for the caravan park owner to sign.

I also found myself having to build a lengthy path and eight pegs around a small circular 'moat style' pond that had been excavated from a much larger loch, more recently used as a boating pond for caravan park residents.

> *Diary Entry, Easter 1993:*
> *This could be a really exciting development with huge*
> *potential for a fishing complex to rival those in*
> *England. I currently await the outcome of water*
> *quality test results as taken by Dr Alistair Stephen the*
> *local fishery scientific officer, vital before introducing*
> *any fish.*

Craichlaw and Glendarroch both fished in their frustratingly unpredictable manner that early spring. At least Culscadden Farm pond gave regular sport even if only for roach and rudd. It was proving its worth as one of the alternatives venues I'd included in the early planning stages. Good Friday saw many unhappy anglers on Craichlaw, including myself, with only Brown trout being caught.

Then suddenly – Bingo! Three of the 'Scottish Carp Group' phoned to tell me that they had landed five carp over their three day stay at Craichlaw, including Mirrors of 18lb and 5lb, a beautiful Common carp of 4lb and two Ghost carp at 3.5lb and 4lb. All were taken off the island, with the 18lb fish tempted by popped-up sweetcorn fished directly underneath lily pads.

18lb.8oz Mirror carp, Craichlaw May '93.

This was typical of the enigmatic and unpredictable nature of Craichlaw Loch. I could bag-up with perhaps ten tench one morning on a dawn session, and fish exactly the same swim using the same method and bait the next dawn only to blank!

In a way it was this that made it such an attractive venue for the visiting anglers. It was nothing like an over-stocked, commercial fishery, where one-eyed fish with frayed lips and net damage were common and the banks were packed with noisy anglers. But boy, it was frustrating!

Hard Work

I signed the deal with the owner of the caravan park and presented my development plan. This included stocking a wide variety of species taken by rod and line from local waters as we awaited the next opportunity to purchase carp and bream stock. I was assured that help would be available to assist me in creating the path around the loch and the flagstone pegs.

I was fortunate that Kev was willing as ever to help me out, because the promised labourer never did turn up! In typical manner, May was warm and sunny; this helped the anglers as carp, tench and bream began to show in increasing numbers. However, the heat didn't help me building a path around the recently enlarged loch. It was very hard and physically draining work, not least because the materials of flagstones, sand, gravel, plastic sheeting etc that were supposed to have been left at various points around the loch hadn't been deposited for me as promised. I had to wheel-barrow them from the reception area right around the entire loch, which of course didn't yet have a path to use for the purpose as I was the one building it. Kev would sometimes turn up after his shift at the butchers. I was very grateful when he did, those flagstones were awful heavy.

Meanwhile, Jackie and I returned to the Birmingham NEC for the National Angling Exhibition '93.

I had learnt from last year, and was much more market specific with my advertising materials. And I booked a different hotel from Dave, so avoided having to sleep in the bath.

Promotional Brochures as distributed at NEC '93.

While I was there, I met one of my childhood angling heroes; Bernard Venables, the UK angling 'treasure' better known to many anglers as 'Mr Crabtree'. He was very approachable amidst the chaos and crowds around us.

"You're the man to blame!" I told him as I approached, smiling, with my hand held out.

"And you're not the first person to accuse me of that!" he responded, jovially. We sat and shared a cup of coffee as I explained how I held him to account for my addiction to angling.

I picked his brains about all matters angling, and he was most forthcoming. He was equally interested by my description of the various waters I controlled, while the notion of fishing for tench in an estate lake in Scotland particularly enticed him.

"If I get the chance, do you think I could fish your waters?" he asked.

I assured Bernard that he would be most welcome. Mr Crabtree fishing my waters? Oh yes! Sadly he never did manage to pay us a visit, passing away in 2001, aged 94.

The milling throngs of anglers at the NEC 1993.

Also at the NEC that year, I met Bob James, one of the co-authors, with Chris Yates, of the book and accompanying TV series *A Passion For Angling*. He signed my copy of the book, and was interested when I explained to him about the plans I had for my fishery and the existing opportunities for carp and tench fishing in Scotland.

Chatting to the very many anglers who stopped at our stall at Angling '93, it was clear just how entrenched anglers' views of fishing in Scotland were. Salmon, trout, pike and perch were associated with Scotland, not carp, bream and tench. This was something I thought about afterwards. Could I turn this into an advantage? For English anglers, catching carp in Scotland might be a possible marketing attraction, a feather in their fishing cap, particularly as 'The Scottish Carp Group' was already in existence. Food for thought as we made the long journey homeward.

Elsewhere in 1993 . . .

Outside the 'bubble' of my new lifestyle, the world was continuing to turn slowly and as unpredictably as ever.

The IRA continued its deadly campaign of bombings across the UK, including the planting of a bomb in Warrington, a town where Jackie and I had once lived happily surrounded by good folk and many friends. Two young boys – Jonathan Ball, aged three years old and Tim Parry, just 12 years old, were murdered, along with 50 other people injured in the blast. Thankfully this bombing eventually emerged as one atrocity too many for all concerned, and proved to be a significant stepping stone on the road to an eventual peace agreement.

Unemployment was finally coming down, with signs that the recession was gradually coming to an end, although Labour remained way ahead of the Tories in the polls.

There was a false start to The Grand National, leading to it being cancelled for the first time ever.

The WRNS ('Wrens'), in which my mother served during WW2, were disbanded, with female sailors henceforth being assimilated into The Royal Navy.

In football, Manchester United won the first ever English Premier League, while the mighty Wigan Athletic were relegated, leading to a heavy drinking session and some tears at a certain guest house in

Newton Stewart, Scotland.

This was the year that Harry Kane and Stormzy were born, but also that Les Dawson and Bobby Moore sadly left us.

The Christmas Number One in the pop charts turned out to be Noel Edmunds with 'Mr Blobby'. I know, I know, tough times on the music front.

Football Scouting

I had been a Wigan Athletic FC fan since the age of 11. It was entrenched deep in my soul. God knows I'd tried to lose the passion and devotion to what was invariably a losing cause, to no avail. (My first book, 'Mild & Bitter Were the Days' is evidence of the pain this caused me!)

While living on Tyneside, I'd undertaken official football scouting duties for Wigan, and I'd recommended a couple of players that went on to have successful careers in the game. Sadly though, none of the players that I recommended were taken on by Wigan Athletic at the time. One of the ones I watched quite a few times without actually forwarding his name was a certain Graham Jones, who did eventually become a firm fans' favourite at Springfield Park. I watched him play a few times when he was 17 or 18 years old, playing for both Newcastle Blue Star FC and later for North Shields FC. He was sent off the first time I watched him play and booked in each game thereafter, which I hope explained my reluctance to formally recommend him. 'Too hot-headed,' I'd written in my notes. He is now a highly successful coach at club and country level and at the time of writing is on duty with the England squad. Not bad for a 'hot-head'.

Who else did I go to watch, following tip-offs over the years? Chris Waddle, playing for Tow Law Town FC was one – 'Too lazy, languid in style and lacks penetration,' I wrote in my notes. Meanwhile, my observations about a certain Paul Gascoigne read, 'Clearly talented, always demanding the ball and has great awareness, but appears a bit overweight and too easily wound-up by the opposition.'

I was clearly never going to make it big as a football scout, but I maintained my interest on moving to Scotland, following all the local teams looking for that elusive 'gem'. One local football 'aficionado' took me to one side in the pub one night, and begged me to go and watch a certain local player. He thought that the lad concerned, who worked behind the bar in my local, had been let go by Glasgow Rangers prematurely and deserved a second chance.

I went along to watch him on a number of occasions. Although clearly talented, he had an attitude problem when things went against him. He was also slow to involve team-mates when he should've done, lacking that all important 'peripheral vision'. Overall, I wasn't convinced that he would make inroads into the Wigan Athletic squad, as bad as they were at the time, and I certainly didn't want to raise his hopes unduly.

I typed up my completed assessment form and went to explain it all to him. He listened to my comments with clear disdain. He then read my report, rolled it into a paper-ball and threw it back at me, hitting me in my face! In a strange way I was grateful; this childish behaviour merely confirmed my suspicions regarding his immature character and unsuitability for a career in professional football.

I continued scouting for a few seasons until Wigan Athletic were taken over by local multi-millionaire Dave Whelan in 1995. His wealth meant that Wigan could sign players of proven experience and ability, as a result of which I'm delighted to say we began our meteoric rise up the English Leagues. Unfortunately this also meant that I eventually received a message from the then-manager Bruce Rioch, suggesting that any player I recommended should be of a sufficient standard to play in the upper echelons of the English Football League.

I hadn't seen anyone of that ability playing in the Scottish Southern Counties League. Nor even The Scottish Leagues two or three, where I had seen many Stranraer FC and Queen of The South games. Gradually my football scouting career came to an end, although my love of Wigan Athletic remains undiminished, and equally painful.

This was probably just as well, as I hopefully had a busy summer of 1993 ahead . . .

A Nod To Rodders

We soon came to realise that in a small town such as Newton Stewart, word of mouth was everything by way of reputation. For all our advertising in national magazines and tourist board outlets for incoming business, if the locals had your business down as naff, then family, friends and businesses looking for accommodation would be guided elsewhere. So we looked to make improvements in our 'brand image' at a local level.

Having attended many of the local football team's matches, I had frequently been asked to sponsor Newton Stewart FC. Davy Frame was one such person urging me to become involved. He was one of the committee men and eventually persuaded me to sponsor a game. I was very reluctant, it seemed like £25 spent on a 90-minute advert actually seen by only 60 fans would be of limited value. He was a good salesman though, and knew my weak spot. "You're from Wigan, aren't you? How about we throw in a pie at half-time and maybe even a cuppa tea?" Davy had me at 'pie', and the deal was done.

The advert consisted of a large, pitch-side advertising hoarding, with the details of the sponsor writ in large letters. This was rolled out on the afternoon of the game and for the pre-match warm up session as the crowd gathered.

I selected a game with most interest, a local derby between Newton Stewart FC and Creetown FC, hoping that a larger than usual crowd would maximise the publicity generated for The Palakona Guest House.

There was indeed a good attendance, with all the pre-match banter and rivalry one might expect. I was quite caught up in it all and enjoying the atmosphere, so much so that I hadn't even noticed the sponsors sign until I realised that some of the humorous comments were being aimed in my direction and a friend pointed me towards the sponsors' signboard. There, in huge letters, catching the eye of all concerned, read:

Today's Match Sponsor is . . .

THE PLONKA GUEST HOUSE

Queen Street

Newton Stewart

402323

I was initially annoyed at the spelling mistake, but when I realised the amount of attention and amusement this spelling error was generating, I was pleased. I have to say that the Scotch pie went down well at half-time, too.

Davy came to see me, apologising profusely and insisting that someone, probably kids, must've been messing about with the lettering after he had set it up earlier that morning. When I heard his slurred voice and smelt his whisky breath, I kind of worked out what had actually occurred.

7 DEVELOPING THE BUSINESS

That summer of 1993 demonstrated to us that with the right development, energy, patience and investment, the fishery could be a lucrative arm of our overall business in its own right and not, as we had perhaps anticipated, merely existing as an add on; an attraction to boost trade for the guest house.

Kev and I fished various local waters that summer, transferring our catches to the newly acquired caravan park water. In one week we managed 61 perch, 67 rudd, and 82 roach, plus two bonus eels. We were keen to provide at least some sport for the early summer anglers booked into the caravan park. As it turned out, we needn't have put so much time and effort in, as the fish farm I ordered from suddenly announced a delivery date in just one week's time.

This stocking saw a wide range of smaller carp, bream, tench and Crucian carp introduced into the caravan park water, as well as into Glendarroch Loch and Craichlaw Loch.

I also put twenty small carp into the recently discovered holding pools at Glendarroch, and fed these regularly as the summer progressed. It was a continuation of 'the buy small and bring them on' policy, as most fish were around the 1lb in weight mark, with a lot of much smaller ones in the mix, too.

Matchmen? Can't tell 'em owt . . .

I had already noted with interest that neither Craichlaw nor Glendarroch responded well to traditional match tactics. It was clear that piling in copious amounts of groundbait into water just 4 feet deep, then wafting poles over, or crashing feeders into, the same swims, invariably spelled disaster. In addition, many angling clubs and groups would insist on shouting loudly across the loch! They would wander around the bank-side noisily chatting to each other and standing visibly on the sky-line having a smoke and laughing loudly, thereby frightening away every fish in the swim. Whenever possible, I would have a chat with the anglers either in the loch-side car-park or, if they were guests, in the guest house prior to heading off to the water, about such matters. I invariably wasted my breath!

The groups that did take my advice would arrange 'split-shift' matches, fishing at dawn and dusk to avoid the bright sunny daytime light levels. They would also adopt a 'softly-softly' approach. If it were possible, they would rake the swims the evening prior, and feed sparing amounts of particles into the selected match swims.

What a difference this made! Tench, carp and bream would invariably show up in addition to the plentiful roach and rudd. Combined dawn and dusk bags would often see match winning bags to be in the 15lb-25lb range. This split-shift idea also left the lads free through the day to explore the many attractions in the area, or more likely to visit the pubs and bookies in town.

Meanwhile, anglers on my other waters were enjoying variable sport as the water temperatures rose and the fish got on the feed in earnest, at least some of the time.

A local angler reported that his son had caught a small (and blind) Well's catfish in Glendarroch, presumably deposited in there from a home aquarium. The poor thing didn't survive long, it was never seen again.

As the summer progressed, Craichlaw was its usual 'Jekyll and Hyde' self, providing superb sport one day then dreadful results the next. However, if you had weather conditions on your side, namely fishing into the prevailing westerly breeze on an overcast and mild day the tench, carp bream and silver fish would give excellent sport.

Glendarroch offered more consistent sport, but the fish were much smaller. Two anglers from Manchester had 26lb of roach, rudd, perch and Crucian carp, plus a 3lb 6oz bream, but the next day they both struggled for 5lb each.

Culscadden Farm Pond continued to provide excellent sport for decent roach and the occasional tench, along with plenty of eels. Being small, it was better suited to families or a limited number of anglers.

While the accommodation levels at The Palakona Guest House were disappointing that summer, the fishing day-ticket sales on all three waters were booming. This posed much food for thought for Jackie and me. We were quickly realising that school-holiday times were not good for our accommodation bookings. But the many family visitors to caravan parks, chalets and self-catering establishments meant that where we lost out in terms of guests, we made up for with fishing activity.

I had started to hire out fishing tackle, as no one else in the area offered this service. It went very well, but I quickly learnt to ask for a deposit as often the tackle would be handed back without any mention of damage that had been sustained! One set of rod, reel and nets were never returned at all, the address given being false. Some folk, eh?

Autumn saw a gradual reduction in trade. Mid-October would be a busy period, but after that it was like dropping off a cliff. This was the perfect opportunity for Jackie to take a well-earned long-weekend break, on this occasion going to London with her friends.

I managed most things in her absence, such as breakfasts, laundry and packed lunches etc, limiting the number of guests to no more than six people per night. However, I wouldn't wish my evening meals upon our guests – we wanted them to return, after all – so my Mum kindly cooked these.

Jackie's absence led to diary entries like the following being written in advance . . .

> *October 24th:*
> *KEN . . . Don't forget to remind the girls to have school clothes ready for tomorrow, especially Emma.*

Stocking

While I eagerly awaited Jackie's return, I was also looking forward to another major stocking of fish. At the end of October they duly arrived.

'Framlingham Fisheries' of Ipswich provided this batch to our ever-expanding fish 'family'. *That's one heck of a journey*, I thought at the time, but they were only two hours late and we proceeded to introduce 600 roach for the caravan park anglers.

Marital Bliss?

The owner of a nearby large house set in its own grounds had heard that I was transporting carp into the area, and asked if he could take advantage of this to buy some ornamental carp for a large garden pond that he had recently drained and de-silted. He left the purchase of these fish to his good lady wife who chose the species, size and price, I kept out of it. The pond renovation was apparently her 'project'.

On the morning of the stocking at the caravan park, he arrived with two household buckets to transfer his newly acquired fish back to the nearby house. It seemed that his wife had been a little economical with the truth when it came to explaining precisely what she had ordered directly from the fish farm. Neither of them appreciated just how large the carp were; I think she expected small goldfish, or Koi. She had actually ordered no less than ten large Mirror carp at a total cost of £250. You couldn't get one of them in his bucket, never mind ten! The poor chap was embarrassed, and I had to lend him both the means to transfer his fish and the use of Kev to demonstrate how they were to be safely and gradually introduced into his large garden pond.

He didn't seem very happy with his acquisition. I'm so pleased I wasn't involved when he and his wife discussed the considerable purchase costs. My parting words to him were "Nowt to do with me, pal ..."

After we'd stocked the caravan park we moved on to Craichlaw Loch, where Mr Knott from Glenwhan Gardens arrived. He had purchased 11 2lb, beautifully marked Koi carp for his ornamental pond. I'd agreed that he, too, could piggy-back on our delivery. Finally, Tony Taylor took 250 small tench to his private waters of 'Drumrae Loch' and 'Cairnhouse Loch'. What an easy touch I was, but my intention was to establish good relations with new friends, neighbours and develop a business network based on goodwill. I reasoned that I was paying delivery costs anyway, so why not?

We stocked Craichlaw with 55 carp, a mixture of Mirrors, Commons and Leathers ranging from 1lb to 4lb, plus two bonus 2lb Koi carp. In addition, we put in 200 bream ranging from 1lb to over 4lb.

We then went across the road to Glendarroch Loch, into which we placed a similar species mix of fish, but fewer in number.

Finally, as the night came in Kev and I took the longer trip to Culscadden Farm Pond, where we tipped 11 small bream and ten carp of about 1lb.

Total cost was £1,230.31. All details faithfully recorded in the diary of the time.

In total I had stocked well over 3,000 fish into the various waters I now controlled since commencing operations in May 1991. This represented a considerable financial investment, but it did mean that we could offer a wide variety of coarse fishing both in terms of venues and species. It also meant that we could budget for the next year or so without having to include fish stocking costs.

Another winter begins

I enjoyed taking advantage of quieter fishing numbers, and would often find myself all alone while fishing, in solitary bliss.

Wrapping up warm was essential, of course, but sometimes it was well worth the effort.

Diary Entry, November 1993:
Kev and I fished Culscadden Farm Pond. Clear and sunny. Nothing showed all afternoon then as dusk set in, 'Bingo!' Perch and roach with every chuck. But . . . there is a very worrying and unexplained drop in water levels?
"Bream On!! I noticed Bream rolling in the deeper swims at Craichlaw one morning. I couldn't resist the call, and was soon ledgering with worms and maggot. In a couple of hours I managed three bream to 4lb various skimmers and a 2lb carp. Very pleased, as I only had garden worms and some scabby maggots and pinkies for bait!"

This, and other similar occasions where bait was in short supply, got me thinking. Often a dangerous thing to allow to happen, in my case.

A Sliding Tackle

As I said earlier, in the years before actually purchasing the business, I knew that the previous owner had set up a fishing tackle shop in what we were using as a guest lounge. His son Richard ran the shop, and it would be hard to find a more helpful chap. He had previously pointed us to productive waters and even specific pegs, especially where pike fishing was concerned; the lad knew his stuff. This proved to be a lesson to me for future reference. Knowledge equals power and influence. Sadly the shop hadn't lasted for very long, but the need for its very existence must have sat within my subconscious, awaiting rebirth.

When we first moved in, I had spoken to both tackle shop owners in town about increasing their range of coarse fishing stock, and also improving the bait supply available. One was lukewarm about both ideas, while the other wasn't interested at all. They both stocked basic gear like pike bungs, disgorgers and bubble floats, but very little else. It was the same story when it came to bait. Maggots and worms were available in limited amounts at Easter and May Bank Holidays or during English school holidays, but they were in very limited supply at all other times.

In one of the shops, 'old Albert' Emerson was a true gentleman, who helped me enormously and was a superb fly-tier but who had little time for coarse anglers. "Gentlemen anglers don't use maggots," he would harrumph. Little did he ever know just how many trout anglers would call in for a tub of maggots, especially when an important competition was due!

The maggots that were stocked weren't cared for well, invariably turning into caster within a short time, sometimes throughout a fishing session! I even had to explain to one of the tackle-shop owners what 'pinkies' were – he thought they were Communist sympathisers, and that 'boilies' were potatoes. Another of them understood a 'pole' to be an east European 'Johnny Foreigner type', or perhaps just an archaic term for a rod. These limitations of awareness applied to sea-fishing too, for which there was virtually no tackle and certainly no bait available.

For many anglers, including myself, there was no alternative other than to travel the 50-mile round trip to Stranraer, or even further to Castle Douglas, to look for tackle and bait, with no guarantee of success.

On one occasion, I phoned the tackle shop in Castle Douglas to check that they had maggots in stock; having been assured that they did, I ordered my two pints. By the time I arrived they'd sold out. The person I'd placed my order with over the phone – the shop owner – hadn't told his colleague, and went out on business, leaving her to sell out of maggots. I wasn't best pleased that day.

I couldn't blame the local tackle shops, really; in their experience, there just wasn't the market to fill their shelves with items that wouldn't sell. Both shops mostly catered for the shooting fraternity and fly-fishing trade, and stocked vast amounts of gear for these locally popular pursuits. I realised I needed to create a need. It was my task to persuade them that I intended to boost the coarse fishing visitors to a point where it would be worth their while to cater for them.

Winter Returns

The winter of 1993/94 came early, with snow appearing on Cairnsmore from the beginning of November. But this didn't stop us from fishing. The local club fished various matches, with my neighbour Eric and his son Stephen having to break the ice at Craichlaw one Sunday morning. Not one angler amongst us caught a single fish!

Another match took place at Culscadden, where four anglers took part on another frosty morning. The match was won with one small perch. It was definitely time to reconsider the viability of this Winter League.

That match did help to eventually solve a riddle, though. As we fished in the perishing cold, I noticed a farmhand arrive with a water-bowser at the back of his tractor and promptly pump out vast amounts of water from the pond as he filled up the bowser. He explained that the stand-pipe water supply to both the farmyard and the byre had frozen solid. This explained why anglers had previously complained about the variable water levels.

Workers' Rights

The cold snap continued throughout November, with temperatures down to minus five degrees Celsius. Most waters were iced over, with very few local anglers willing to fish them.

I used the time to build platforms at Glendarroch Loch. I paid £120 for pressure treated timber, which then had to be relocated to various points around the loch. The frozen surface meant that I couldn't float rafts of the stuff across the loch as I'd planned, and I had to carry it around what was a wide and increasingly treacherous perimeter.

Construction was a laborious effort, in bitterly cold conditions. The planks of wood had to be literally hammered apart each morning, as they had frozen overnight. I had to break the surface ice in order to pile-drive the base support stobs into the loch base using a mell. The condensation and sweat froze on my clothes, while my fingers frequently slipped off the nails and off the mell as I slithered around underfoot in the icy water. I had black fingernails for weeks. *Who needs nail-varnish or a pedicurist?*, I mused.

I must have been crazy working under such conditions. Where was the Health and Safety Act when you needed it? Where was my union rep? Who was the boss I'd need to speak to about a 'duty of care'? Oh, hang on . . .

It took most of the week, many painful fingers and a sore back to complete the work, but I managed to construct eight fishing platforms and fix anti-slip mesh to them all. I then took the top and bottom of a few tin cans, painted them white with black numbering, and fixed them to each platform, to allocate pegs for match draws. I was quite proud of my efforts, all things considered.

On a negative note, however, I also noticed three small carp frozen into the impenetrable ice at Craichlaw Loch. As beautiful as she can appear to be, Mother Nature can be harsh, too.

Winter at Craichlaw Loch, 1993.

Shooters' Surprise Return
As the Salmon season ended on the various local rivers and coarse

anglers were in short supply, so our other target group (excuse the pun), the shooters, started to arrive. We had learnt from previous years. Our advertising had been much more specific this time around, and we had managed to build on our return trade. But while the inland wildfowlers came in increasingly good numbers as the month progressed, we still relied on miscellaneous customers to make ends meet.

We also had forestry workers stay with us, who were in the area to cut down thousands of young conifers for the Christmas tree market. Who knew that Christmas trees were cut down in late October and early November? We also had some life-saving trade from workers labouring on a gas pipeline being installed right across Dumfries and Galloway.

A few hardy pike anglers risked frozen waters to come to stay, but not many. Overall, we had to live off savings from busier periods of the year, and on many nights the guest house was empty. The early part of December saw inland shooters numbers diminish and our overall accommodation numbers fall worryingly. Passing trade was very low as people presumably saved their pennies for Christmas. This period proved to be the nadir of our business; if it had got much worse we'd have had to sell up and return to Tyneside with our tails between our legs.

This wasn't a viable long-term business model.

Jackie took this opportunity to take the kids to visit family and friends on Tyneside, and to do some Christmas shopping. She had barely been gone a few hours when news of geese arriving in good numbers on the foreshore saw the telephone never stop ringing as wildfowlers started to book in. Just as Percy Betts had suggested, the geese would decide when trade would pick up, and he was right! My Mum kindly came to the rescue to help with breakfasts and evening meals in Jackie's absence. I could've managed on my own, though. Of course I could . . .

Business remained fairly steady right up to Christmas Day. We closed again on Christmas Eve but had to re-open on Boxing Day evening when, due to a booking mix-up on their part, a group of shooters turned up, with dogs, expecting accommodation. We knew nothing of this until their pick-up truck startled us by pulling into the car park at the rear and they started disembarking guns, holdalls and dogs accompanied by warm, hearty Christmas greetings.

Jackie and I just stared at each other as our jaws dropped. I dashed upstairs to turn on the bedroom heating, light the fire in the guests' lounge and set the tables.

Poor Jackie meanwhile had to somehow magic up evening meals for four people on Boxing Day. Of course she managed it, as ever. I can't quite recall what the meal consisted of, but I could hazard a guess it involved turkey.

As 1993 waved goodbye and 1994 arrived, the misgivings we were experiencing about the viability of the accommodation side of the business was nothing compared to the disaster that hit what I had now officially termed 'Craichlaw Fisheries', and in particular Craichlaw Loch . . .

8 'THE CRAICHLAW FISHERIES OTTER-FEEDING SERVICE'

Diary Entry, December 1993:
Andrew phoned to tell me that his wife, Mary had
found a dead fish on the dam wall and on
investigation, sure enough – a Mirror carp of 8lb-
10lb, very dead. Only the head, tail and parts of the
body remained, with scales scattered all around. On
closer inspection there was clear evidence of atrophied
eggs present.
Alistair Stephen (Local Fisheries Scientific Officer)
thinks it is an otter death, but the atrophied eggs
made us wonder if this wasn't a factor in this fish's
demise too. Was it failing, spawn-bound or even dead
when the otter found it?

As 1994 dawned I discovered a succession of dead carp at Craichlaw and, to a lesser extent, Glendarroch. In the first three weeks I found 12 dead carp varying in size between 4lb and 9lb. Many hadn't been de-scaled at all, there was no sign of the fish being taken for food, just large bite wounds, often a chunk of flesh taken from around the neck then the carcass left to rot. A number of the carp I found were floundering at the bank-side in mortal agony, left to die a slow and painful death. I was forced to dispatch them as an act of mercy. Even the small carp placed in the holding ponds for 'bringing on' hadn't escaped the otter's attention, very few were left alive.

This was a disastrous state of affairs, undoing all the good work I'd put in, potentially damaging our reputation and ruining the financial investment involved in stocking. It simply couldn't go on.

I researched the issue, seeking advice from various sources including fishing literature, local anglers, and other coarse fisheries. I also had lengthy conversations with the ever helpful Dr Alistair Stephens, and with Don Patterson at The Barony College. Finally, and in desperation, I contacted the local 'Otter Rehabilitation Centre' at nearby Barrhill.

Amongst everything I picked up during the course of my enquiries, the key points I learned were as follows:

a) Carp can re-absorb spawn, but if they fail to do so successfully, likely due to cold water conditions, they can suffer from a toxic re-absorption syndrome, which is often fatal.

b) Otters are highly successful scavengers who will seek food of any kind from wherever they can find it. They prefer eels, trout, crayfish and even salmon, but if these are seasonally not available while big, fat, semi-dormant carp are, they will readily take the carp. Furthermore, the instinct to kill often outweighs the urge to eat.

c) Carp were likely to have borne the brunt of the otter attacks as Tench, and eels are more adept at hiding in the silt and root mass. They do not foolishly wave their tails around, unlike the barely awake or aware carp, which attracts the attentions of any passing inquisitive otter with such behaviour.

d) Otters are a protected species and as such NO steps could be taken to disturb them or the environment in which they've set up residence.

Frankly, I wished I'd never asked . . .

The otter expert, a certain Mr Jim Green, undertook a full assessment and reported that our otter had set up base in a quiet corner of Glendarroch Loch. Furthermore, angling activity could be seen as disturbing the otter's natural environment and thus arguably should be suspended forthwith. My counter-argument was that the bloody thing was only here *because* of the angling activity, seeking the same quarry that I had stocked and paid for! While the fishery worked hard to stock fish, the otter worked equally hard to kill them, often merely for fun! I appreciated that I was on dodgy moral ground with this argument, but even so I wasn't a happy chappy.

To be fair, Mr Green did advise me to ensure I kept within the law. He reminded me that I certainly couldn't poison, shoot, net or trap the otter. Neither could I interfere with or invade its lair, or 'holt', and he advised me to seal off the nearest fishing platforms to prevent this happening by accident. Finally, he suggested that I should perhaps try to accept the presence of the otter as a much loved and threatened species, to be valued as "an added attraction to the natural local environment."

Aye, that'll be right!

Throughout January and February, almost any cold, frosty night would see at least one dead carp being discovered on the bank-side. Some mornings three or four very dead, but barely touched, fish would emerge. I wondered morosely just how many carcasses were floating in the copious weed beds, never to be found.

My reading around the issue threw up an interesting suggestion, and one that I had the means to put into practice. Apparently, otters have a healthy respect for and fear of dogs, consequently avoiding areas that dogs frequent. I had kennels full of straw that was soaked in dog urine, from the dogs belonging to our guest shooters.

I spent hours undertaking the smelly job of collecting the bedding, then slowly and methodically spreading it around the bank-side of Glendarroch and Craichlaw Lochs. I intentionally avoided the far end of Glendarroch, where Jim Green had pointed out the otters had set up home, to complying with the advice given and avoid any potential legal issues.

I'm delighted to say that it worked! Well, up to a point. For a full month following this deterrent exercise there were no more carp deaths and no further sightings of the vicious beast; I was delighted and relieved in equal measure.

Sadly, my relief proved to be premature. Towards the end of March 1994, as temperatures suddenly plummeted, the otter returned to its wicked ways, plundering another six carp. These deaths almost always took place at Craichlaw, yet we knew the otter lived at Glendarroch – another strange quirk of the entire episode.

The carnage was having a direct and negative effect on the fishery's reputation. Our regular carp anglers would phone and ask if we'd got rid of the otter, or ask in 'jest' whether there were any carp left for fishing. One guest and his wife went to fish Craichlaw and found four large carp carcasses on the island. They came back and checked out immediately.

I spoke to Andrew Gladstone; he was the owner of the affected waters after all, and I leased the fishing rights from him. I also sought further advice from the Otter Sanctuary. The former was as helpful and sympathetic as ever, the latter less so.

I estimated that I had lost £350 worth of carp, and in recognition of this Andrew kindly agreed to a temporary extension to the lease payment. Jim Green at the Otter Sanctuary suggested that I could only hope that as the seasons progressed the otter would return to its' more usual hunting grounds of local rivers, burns and the foreshore. "But," he warned me, "they have long memories." I forlornly spread more urine-stained straw.

However, more human activity in the form of anglers on the waters, along with the change in the seasons, combined to see an end to the carp deaths. It wasn't entirely the last I'd see of the otter, though . . .

One evening, later that summer, I'd been fishing off the island at Craichlaw Loch and as darkness fell I began to pack up my gear. As I went into the water to retrieve my bank-stick an otter swirled, sat up on its haunches just inches from me, and loudly chattered in my direction. I think it was swearing at me. I know I was swearing at him.

I was in shock with heart palpitations. Just how long it had been in the immediate vicinity of my swim I don't know, but it clearly resented my presence in what it perceived to be its territory.

Some weeks later, Digger and I were checking out Glendarroch Loch for day-ticket avoiding anglers and their inevitable litter, when I noticed energetic activity out in the reed-mace. Digger noticed it too, and started barking. Sure enough, out of the weeds emerged a large and very confident dog otter that swam powerfully straight towards us. Digger couldn't resist the challenge, and leapt into the water to do battle with this intruder into his perceived domain. I knew what the inevitable outcome would be, and I was fearful for Digger's safety. He hadn't seen the size of an otter's teeth, nor their fearsome agility in the water, like I had. I shouted and whistled loudly, imploring him to come back to me, which thankfully he eventually did. Both adversaries seemed to feel that this show of strength formed an honourable draw, and both withdrew from the field of potential battle with their pride intact.

This episode signalled the end of the otter problem as a major issue. As the year went by, I would still occasionally find otter spraint along the bank-side, but on closer examination it would consist of small, fine bones, as if it had targeted the smaller silver fish.

Very few dead carp were discovered by me or any of our visitors, and even when an occasional sighting was reported I was often convinced it was Mink. I can only surmise that the otter moved on to pastures new, having found an even richer source of protein than Craichlaw carp, or possibly even a mate.

Old Friends Return

While the otter was running wild at Craichlaw Fisheries, the Palakona Guest House was going through a post-festive period of quiet, with virtually no bookings for the first nine days of 1994.

But just as Percy Betts had forecast, as the geese filled the foreshore, so the shooters filled our guest house. By early January, familiar names appeared in the booking diary and friendly faces appeared at the door. Dave Harris and the London boys, the Salford lads, Jimmy, Russell,

Terry and Co were all regulars and always welcome. They were amiable, funny, honest and came for many years. Some of them put down roots in the town that continue to this day.

Other groups came from all over the UK, with Leicestershire in particular seeming to have a lot of wildfowlers. Perhaps being inland meant that the coast had an extra attraction. Many were return bookings from the previous two winters, and it was a pleasure and a relief to see them all.

Russell from Salford and his two geese 'under the moon'.

Dog on guard, a mixed bag from a good weekend's shooting.

Ups and Downs

Diary Entries, February 1994:
I've re-negotiated the lease for Craichlaw, Glendarroch and Spa Wood lochs with Andrew who kindly agreed to help pay for lost carp. Replace with tench I think.
I want to settle matters with the caravan park owner. Apparently he isn't happy with our deal. He didn't turn up!
I've been approached by a Mrs Kirk to manage her fishery in Creetown and at a later date, the salmon and pike fishing on the stretch of the River Bladnoch that she and her husband own.
I've been and checked out the loch at Creetown, it is an excellent water. Good PH, spring fed, 8–12 feet deep, could easily accommodate 30 match anglers and there is even a car-park!
I went for a chat and a coffee at the house where she dominated matters and her husband kept strangely quiet. I've left them a package of information and suggestions on coarse fishing and I hope that she'll plump for that rather than just trout.

(Sadly no progress was made. I was given to understand that her husband took not well and as a result any developments were put on hold.)

I've pulled out of the deal with the caravan park. The owner felt that he would do better by himself and that he wanted to increase the rent from the agreed £250 p.a. to an unspecified amount to be negotiated annually. In addition he wanted to retain 100% of all day-ticket monies taken! Err, what in it for me? I questioned. "We'll send anglers to you for bait and tackle . . ." was his reply. I thought to myself, 'But they'll have to come to me anyway. I'm the only tackle supplier in the area that caters for coarse anglers and their tackle and bait needs!"

Basically he had got what he wanted. He used me to create a fishery out of a boating pond for his caravan park only to then make the lease conditions such that I had no choice but to pull out.

I'm angry, I feel used and stupid at being duped so easily. I blame myself, I had suspicions from the start and I was warned by others to be careful with this chap. The signs were there too. He wouldn't have our initial agreement typed up let alone sign it. He never answered my calls and failed to attend an arranged meeting to sort it all out. He had even wanted each individual fish counted when we originally stocked the loch!

On the other hand, the loch was far from my idea of how fishing should be. It could be noisy. Maintenance was considerable because of the holidaying families with their bikes, inflatable boats, litter, and bank-side fires. It also has a resident otter, Oh the irony!

On the plus side this leaves me with £250 to invest elsewhere in our business, possibly a new water perhaps? I have an idea . . .

With hindsight, I think I was just too keen to get into the holiday park related fishery business, in this case via a caravan park. The potential was tremendous, but it was not for me on this occasion, at least, not with this particular caravan park and its owner.

Meeting a Need

As the year progressed and anglers began to appear from all over the UK and abroad, the need for a reliable bait supply service became imperative. Equally, the dearth of coarse fishing tackle in the two local tackle shops became an increasing problem.

One of the two tackle shops in town initially tried to help. We agreed that I would itemise the tackle I thought I could sell, he would order it in, and I would sell it from the guest house, splitting what little profit there might be. Sounds simple? Sadly it proved not simple enough.

Much of the tackle ordered didn't arrive or simply wasn't as requested. For example, I would ask for barbless hooks-to-nylon in sizes 18 and 20, but they would arrive as loose hooks, barbed, and in size 16 only! The difference in meaning of the word 'Leads' between game-anglers and coarse or sea-anglers led to much confusion, too. As did the different sports being catered for – not many carp anglers had a use for drilled bullets, while this particular shop did sell actual bullets to its shooting clientele.

There were two main markets for the tackle and bait I needed. One was the holidaymaker wanting to dabble at 'fishing for pleasure', while the other was the serious coarse and sea angler. There was a clear increase in the number of both kinds of angler to our region, and I urged the tackle shop owner to respond to this.

I tried selling dead-baits at a series of pike matches that I sponsored. Many of the pike anglers and I were appalled at the dreadful lack of care we observed in a minority of the other competitors in their handling of the fish. Too many anglers used barbed trebles, and too few used landing mats. Some didn't use landing nets at all, preferring to just drag their catch up the rocky bank-side. One pike angler walked all the way round Loch Heron to the weigh-in station with five small pike dangling on a thin string run through their gills as they flapped their tales pitifully. Pike are a surprisingly delicate species, and none survived. I checked the entry form and had to concede that the rules did not state that only live fish could be weighed in. This angler won the match with five dead pike and left with the £100 prize money in his pocket.

The rules were changed thereafter, but the fish handling didn't improve much. In addition to these issues, catches were poor, it was usually perishing cold weather and I didn't sell many dead-baits, let alone tackle.

I eventually pulled out of involvement with organised pike matches. Pike competitions do remain popular in the area to this day, however, and I'm pleased to say that the fish handling is much improved and is usually up to PAC (Pike Angling Club UK) standards.

Contrived Confusion

Around this time, one incident in particular finally forced me into action regarding bait and tackle supply. This occurred when I arranged for an order of both tackle and bait for a Glasgow-based fishing club that had booked in for a weekend of fun and fishing. They ordered worms, maggots, dead-baits, small hooks-to-nylon, crystal wagglers, ground-bait, and a variety of flavoured ground-bait additives. It all amounted to a tidy sum. I ordered it all well in advance through the tackle shop, as per our usual arrangement, and confirmed this with the angling club concerned. You can guess what happened can't you, reader?

Despite numerous frantic requests as the guests' arrival day rapidly approached and equally numerous confirmative reassurances, the order didn't turn up. I had to contact the trip organiser on the morning they were due to arrive. I apologised profusely and suggested that perhaps they could call in to their usual tackle shop at home before they set off to buy the various items? Unfortunately they were travelling in separate cars and not all of them got the message as there were very few mobile phones around in those days. On arrival I donated what I could from my personal tackle and bait fridge, while the lads rationed out the limited amount of maggots and worms they'd managed to purchase on route.

I was furious with the local shop-owner, who merely shrugged his shoulders and nonchalantly blamed the supplier, his shop assistant, and the courier – indeed, anyone except himself. In hindsight, I suspect that he omitted the order on purpose or hadn't followed up on my many urgent phone calls, by way of a shot across my bows. Perhaps he felt I was getting just a bit too big for my boots, that I was demanding too much from him, and that I should learn to know my place.

Certainly, the order never did arrive, thus confirming my suspicions. This was the final straw for me, so I took action.

Palakona Bait Supplies is Born

The purchase of the guest house included what was optimistically called a 'chalet'. This was located to the rear of the guest house, down the small side alley that gave access to the rear of ours and our neighbour's property. It had been used in the past as a barber shop and newsagents. The previous owner told us that when the guest house was very busy, he would use the building as an overspill, and that he had slept in it himself on occasion. During our initial negotiations to purchase the guest house, we noted that this building had no planning permission for residential use. We learned later that it had no permission for use as a shop, either, despite its previous use over many years as just that!

The building had an electrical power supply, but this had been cut off. There was no gas supply, no toilet and no heating, either; even the water supply had been turned off. Rainwater poured into the building and had done for years, causing damp and structural damage. It was a mess – less of a chalet, more of a shell. We used it as a storage shed for garden tools and suchlike. People had slept in it? Not for long, nor often, I doubted!

A Bait and Tackle Service Emerges

Peter Skimming from 'Skimming and Son Builders' with his co-worker Johnny Milligan alongside him to keep him right, set about renovating this derelict 'chalet' and within weeks had created a very smart, if small, shop. We couldn't afford professional shopfitters to fit the place out, but I gradually built shelving and acquired various point-of-sale display units. I was donated a lovely glass counter and an ancient till that operated with the vicious nature of the infamous till in the BBC TV programme, *Open All Hours*.

Further essential items, such as a deep-freeze unit for dead-baits and various bait-fridges, were acquired from salvage yards or skips, and miraculously brought back to working life. I installed a fish tank stocked with tiny rudd, minnows and newts. This was intended as a display attraction for the youngsters who would feed the residents with maggots or bread-crumb.

Peter Skimming working on the bait and tackle shop, during and after.

After the renovation and fitting out of the shop, we gradually built up the stock levels. Our budget was very tight. We had little money to invest in stock that would only sit on the shelf, so I was careful in what I purchased. Groundbait and additives were popular. I eventually had to buy 25 kilo sacks of groundbait and breadcrumb, then bag them into small amounts for ease of sale. I would boil up hemp and sell it bagged too. Sweetcorn of various hues and flavours was also in great demand, and available nowhere else in the locale.

By far the most popular items we sold in those early days of trading were baits. We shifted maggots by the gallon, and worms of various kinds, plus containers to keep such baits in. Frozen dead-baits for the pike and sea-anglers barely had time to settle in the freezer. The most popular pike baits were mackerel, smelt, sprat, eel section, herring and lamprey. The sea-anglers went for crab, sand-eel and squid. It wasn't long before we were providing live rag worm and lug worm too.

Start-up promotional poster; credit to John Irvine.

At this early stage in developing the bait supply business, we enjoyed a relatively cordial relationship with the fishing tackle shop that I had previously tried to work with, despite our previous fall outs. They sent coarse and sea anglers to me, I sent game anglers and shooters to them.

The other tackle shop refused to acknowledge my existence, though. Sometimes our guests would call in to their shop and ask if there was any coarse fishing or bait to be had locally, just to see what the response would be. The advice they received was to fish the local Forestry Commission waters for pike and perch, but that there was no carp or tench fishing to be had in the vicinity. As for sea fishing or pike baits? Well, the nearest supplier would be Stranraer. Charming! Needless to say, we didn't send any trade their way, either. The owner actually came from Blackpool, and I wasn't surprised therefore to see his window display lights frequently left on overnight.

Jackie and I usually staffed the shop ourselves, although we did take on a part-time assistant during very busy periods. I rigged up a doorbell linked to the guest house should customers need serving when we were busy. It worked quite well in the early stages, but with the fishery business increasing, accommodation picking up and a shop to run, we were certainly kept occupied.

Watching Jackie use tweezers to extract rag-worm from their delivery packs having discovered that they could bite, proved a source of great amusement for many sea-anglers. They travelled in large numbers just to witness the event.

Busted!

Becoming 'trader-wise' wasn't easy for an absolute novice like me, and I was tested by a group of local youngsters aged perhaps 12-13 years old. They would come in on Saturday mornings and buy a tub of worms between them. This involved me having to go into the bait storage room, thus briefly being out of sight of the main shop. (This was a shop design-fault that was soon rectified by the use of a strategically placed wall mirror.) While rummaging in the bait fridge I could hear muttering and whispering, and soon suspected what was happening.

The next time this group came in I went to go to get the worms as usually then suddenly stepped back into the shop area, where I found two of the group filling their pockets with lead weights and hooks! The little rascals were caught lead-handed.

Having heard one of them use their pal's name the week before, I used it to imply that I knew all their names.

"Douglas isn't it? I ken your Mother," I began.

"And you, lad," I added, pointing at another one of the group. "I've seen you at the school, haven't I?" I picked up the phone receiver, and explained that we now had two options: I could either call the police, or we could sort it out here and now between us. This ploy hit the mark, and they shame-facedly emptied their pockets onto the counter, some of them near to tears. I told them to leave, and to only come back in the future with their parents present if they wanted to buy anything – it was up to them to explain to their parents why this was the case!

Later that afternoon two of them did indeed return, accompanied by their parents. As they came down the alley and approached the shop door I braced myself for what I feared was to come, expecting to be accused of falsely vilifying their little darlings. I couldn't have been more wrong. It transpired that both youngsters had gone home and tearfully come clean, admitting to their parents what had happened earlier in the day. Both sets of parents were angry and embarrassed. "We're no bringing up a thief in oor hoose," they assured me, and offered money in recompense. They told me that the two errant rascals were grounded from fishing for an entire month.

I thanked them for coming to see me, but suggested that we all recognise the children's eventual honesty in voluntarily coming clean. Perhaps this act of contrition should go some way in easing the punishment? Apparently my plea for clemency worked, as they were both back in the shop a couple of weeks later. Oh, how they laughed, not, when I shouted from the bait room . . . "I'm watching you!"

As I write this text, those 'kids' are now adults in their late 30s, with families of their own. I exchange drinks and winks in the pub with some of them when we see each other. I like to think that their kids have been brought up not to go shop-lifting!

Mass Escape

I'd been furnished with the secret recipe (or chemical process) required to turn maggots into preserved caster, and was most certainly the only tackle shop that I knew of in South West Scotland that could do this. Some people managed this by simply keeping their maggots for too long, of course.

One club trip from Glasgow had brought their bait with them and had over-estimated the amount they needed. This would occasionally happen, and having checked its condition I would usually buy it from them either to sell in the shop as maggots, or more usually to turn into the highly sought-after caster.

Having enjoyed their weekend away fishing and before leaving for home, these particular lads, (Milton Angling Club, you know who you are!), went for a session in the local pub. It was a sunny but showery day, and the bored 'nominated driver' remained with us, knowing that the assurance given that they would only be out for half an hour was highly unlikely to be honoured.

On their return some two hours later I could hear shouts of alarm, distress and laughter. I rushed out to the front of the guest house to where their van was parked up. To my horror I discovered a veritable sea of pinkies, squats and multi-coloured maggots marching out of the back of their van, across the pavement and up the wall of our long-suffering neighbour's house. This was the excess bait that the anglers had hoped to sell on to me; I wondered if the bait suspected their collective fate and had made a bold bid for freedom?

Thousands upon thousands of them had clearly been escaping for a while. They glistened in the sunshine, gaining traction from the damp wall like a wriggling cloak of many colours as they climbed up ever higher, until they were able to make their way across bedroom window-panes. Thank God the windows were closed.

Our neighbours Eric and June took it very well, all things considered. Eric emerged first, triumphantly waving the wand of a pressure-hose, and started to blast the escapees with purpose and pleasure. Jackie and I, plus June and her kids, Stephen and Jane, all formed a brush squad, sweeping the critters into the gutter and thence into the drain. The driver sat in the cab, shaking his head in despair. The guilty anglers, full of drink, were falling about laughing and giggling barely able to speak let alone help. Quite how Eric didn't turn the hose on them and indeed us, I'll never know. It must have all formed quite a tableau for any passer-by.

A short time after this incident, Eric and June announced that they had sold their house and were moving to Stirling, a long way away.

They assured us that this decision was entirely as a result of promotion at work for Eric, but to this day I do wonder.

9 BUSY DAYS

Further Reflections

So, here we were, nearly three years into our quest for a new lifestyle, and I was still questioning the wisdom of what we had done.

No day was the same as the last; there were new challenges to face, and fresh issues to wrestle with. We had completely refurbished The Palakona Guest House, inside and out, though there was always more to be done. Craichlaw Fisheries was developing nicely, while The Palakona Bait & Tackle Supplies operation was up and running. Despite all this, the overall business was still not making much overall profit. But then again, I reasoned, we hadn't entered into this to make large profits.

Our two daughters had settled into their respective schools, and showed ominous signs of leanings toward further education and professional callings having achieved solid, if not spectacular, school reports. They had made good friends, and overall seemed as content as any young teenagers can be (being happy is not part of the deal at that age).

Jackie and I had been welcomed into the local community, and we too had made good friends, particularly in my case amongst the locals of various pubs.

We saw a lot of my Mum and Stepfather, Tom, without either

couple overcrowding the other. We were able to maintain our links with family and friends from our previous life. But I still had reservations (no pun intended).

It was very hard work, and we barely found a minute together for ourselves as a family. And of course, the harder we worked, the more successful we became, which in turn meant we became even busier still! It was a treadmill; we felt like hamsters in a wheel, spinning round and round. And I can't think of a clearer way to illustrate the situation than with the story of my brother Mark's wedding.

Jackie's Wedding Day Blues

The date of my youngest brother's wedding was approaching rapidly. Jackie had chosen her outfit, including the mandatory fancy hat. My daughters had selected and bought their posh frocks, too. We were looking forward to it as an opportunity to share in a joyous family occasion, and to catch up with old friends. At least, we were until two weeks beforehand, when a squad of 12 sea anglers telephoned to book in for four nights. This was worth over £900 in accommodation and meals alone. There would be significant profits from bait and tackle to add to that sum, too. We simply couldn't afford to lose that amount of income.

Jackie bravely volunteered to forego the wedding. Delivering twelve breakfasts, evening meals, packed lunches and bait provisions was a tall order. But with the help of her friend Angela, she managed it. What a star my wife Jackie was (and still is, he says hurriedly). This proved to be a pivotal moment in our venture, however, giving us both much food for thought as to the original purpose behind our lifestyle change.

I took my two daughters to the wedding in Whitley Bay, where we enjoyed ourselves with much Dad dancing and a certain amount of alcohol taken on my part – just to be sociable, of course. It was a wonderful couple of days away, for some of us.

Honestly, Officer!

On the return journey, I collected a consignment of four gallons of maggots from the supplier to bring back for sale in the shop, only to be stopped by the traffic police. I'd been travelling at 68 mph in a 60 mph zone. It was a quiet Sunday evening on an almost deserted A75, and I reckon the Bobbies were just bored. In my defence, I was in a hurry to get the maggots back and into the fridge before they overheated which, judging by the smell in the car, was well on the way to happening.

It was almost worth the fine just to see the traffic cop's face when he asked me why I was in such hurry. "Erm . . . I need to get my maggots back quickly officer," I explained. I bet he hadn't heard that excuse before. He looked at me wide-eyed, thinking I was winding him up, and insisted that I show him the maggots in the boot. This was a decision he instantly regretted as I opened up the containers. He rapidly replaced the container lids and closed the boot with a loud slam, before the stench of ammonia overpowered him. I didn't think police officers were meant to swear on duty. The ticket was issued in record time and I was sent on my way. Oh, the joys.

Sea Fishing

I'd turned my hand to sea fishing in the past, but never considered myself an expert; banging out cod off Blyth Pier or from Whitley Bay beach was the best I could claim. But I was fortunate to have a few pals who were eclectic in their choice of angling; irritatingly skilful anglers who could turn their hand to various forms of fishing. Local Andy Everett was one of these. He could catch trout fly-fishing, big pike on dead-baits, carp and tench on boilies, or land tope and sea-bass, though not all of them always on the same day. Andy was always helpful in guiding me and thus our guests and shop customers to the most productive marks.

The late and greatly missed Tony Taylor was another all-rounder who became a firm friend. Tony lived for fishing. No matter the weather, he would be found sat at the side of Craichlaw Loch, or enjoying sport on his own private lochs, or hunkered down behind convenient rocks while shore fishing.

Tony knew the various sea-fishing shore marks better than anyone, and kindly offered to compile a sea-fishing guide for us. This proved to be accurate, useful, and very popular. I sold countless copies in the shop, where the guide and map saved many lengthy explanations and poring over maps by bewildered and perplexed sea-anglers.

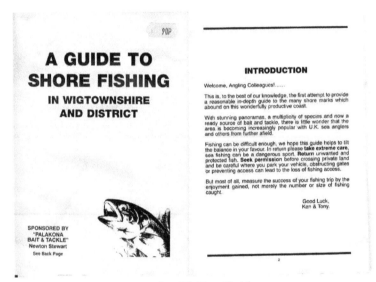

Sea-Fishing Guide.

While species such as whiting, pollack, mullet, codling and sea-bass could be all caught shore fishing, Wigtown Bay and Luce Bay also enjoyed boat-fishing, famously for tope. An annual 'Tope Festival' provided the opportunity for sport and science to work together, as a 'catch, tag and release' programme enabled the marine scientists to better understand this powerful but under threat member of the shark family.

We were fortunate that the skipper of a local commercial sea-fishing operation lived in Newton Stewart. Rab McReadie (RIP) provided sea-fishing trips out of the Isle of Whithorn on his boat the 'M.V. Crusader'. He was a largely jovial character, who knew the local waters well. He could tell you which mark to fish, on what tide, at what time of the year and what baits to use; Rab was a walking encyclopaedia of all matters regarding sea-fishing.

Rab and I enjoyed a mutually beneficial arrangement whereby we exchanged contact details for boat-trips in return for accommodation and bait. This worked well for a few years, although the tides, and thus departure times, led to many early morning breakfast times or late evening meals for Jackie and me to provide!

I shared a few nights of conviviality with Rab in the local pub, The MacMillan Inn, and I was very sorry to hear of his passing in a tragic motorcycle accident some years later.

'Everybody conger . . .'

*The late Rab McCreadie left, with
some happy anglers.*

Mixed Bags

The various waters that constituted Craichlaw Fisheries continued to prove enigmatic. Fantastic catches of tench and bream, and carp to 9lb were frequently reported from anglers at Craichlaw Loch, yet a sudden change in weather could see the very same people blank. Culscadden Farm Pond, despite it being only small, proved one of the more consistent waters. Roach, perch and tench were frequently caught with bags of between 10lb to 15lb often recorded on the returned day tickets.

There was a mysterious 'beast' in Culscadden pond that was never actually landed. The anglers fishing Culscadden tended to fish with light tackle and small hooks for lots of relatively small fish. Consequently a carp, or a large tench, or possibly even a big eel, would smash them up, leaving many tales of the one that got away. I had it on myself once; I played it for five minutes and it felt big – powerful, and heavy. I almost managed to get a fleeting glimpse of it as it came to the net, only for it to surge away and come off the hook. To this day I wonder what it was.

The tackle shop was proving to be very popular indeed. Trade had rocketed in a couple of months, with takings of £200 to £300 per week being recorded on a regular basis. While this was wonderful news, it did keep me tied to the shop. Riddling maggots, ordering replacement stock of tackle and bait, and serving in the shop was all very trying, and meant I had less time for bailiffing duties.

HMRC (The Tax Man/Lady Cometh)

We received a phone call from our accountant to say HMRC had been in touch asking for information about our business and tax submissions. We learnt a long time later that an anonymous tip-off had alerted HMRC that we were grossing far, far more than we were admitting to in our audited accounts. We certainly were not.

Despite being certain of our innocence, this was a very worrying period for us; the arrival of a huge tax demand to be paid immediately (HMRC rarely offer repayment terms) would have been catastrophic for the business, and would have meant the immediate end of our adventure. It was a preposterous notion in the first place. We were only just making ends meet. We paid all the taxes asked of us. Our accounts were duly audited each year, and at considerable expense too, I might add.

The woman leading the investigation went into the minutest of detail. For example, she asked questions like, "What proportion of the breakfast cereals were used for guests, and what was used for the family?" and "On a weekly basis, how frequently is the car used for personal use, and how much is it used for business?" She even wanted to know how much washing detergent was used to wash the guest's laundry as opposed to the family's underwear! The tax official interviewed Jackie in the company of our accountant. Poor Jackie was so worried by the whole affair she ended up in tears, which I can assure you is not something she is prone to.

We submitted monthly returns of income and outgoings, and our accountant helped in every way he could. But for many months a large, black cloud hung over us with no sign of it clearing. We were struggling to make a go of this business already; it just seemed so unfair that on top of everything we should be subject to such a detailed enquiry for absolutely no reason. I was angry more than anything. We'd done nothing wrong, played everything by the book, yet we were being persecuted by what was increasingly appearing to be a personal mission. This particular tax official seemed to be unwilling to accept that she had got things wrong and should back off. It was as if to do so would be seen as a professional black mark on her CV.

Then one day, without warning, we heard from our accountant that the investigation was closed. No explanation from the tax official herself, no apology, no written confirmation letter, nothing at all. This led to a mixture of great relief and extreme anger on our part.

A year or so later we heard on the local grapevine that the original allegation of tax impropriety was actually aimed at another guest house proprietor in the town altogether. It had all been a case of mistaken identity. To our certain knowledge he was never subsequently investigated. As the Americans would say, "Go figure . . ."

'My Old Man's A Bin Man'

One of the jobs I couldn't ask Kev to help with was the onerous and smelly task of emptying the rubbish bins. I had inherited a series of large open oil drums situated at various points around Craichlaw Loch that acted as litter bins. There were none around any of my other waters, and this fact caused me to notice a strange quirk of human behaviour. It is a quirk that has recently been noticed by the local Regional Council, as it happens, and applied to the majority of the regions lay-bys. In general, if there are litter bins available people – in my case, anglers – fill them, whereas if none are available they will take their litter home.

This was not always the case, of course. I would sometimes find discarded empty beer cans, tins of sweetcorn, worm tubs and bread wrappers. One regular visitor (you know who you are, Dave) would leave the cellophane wrappers from his cigars scattered around his peg. I even found a five pound note once; I saw this as a generous tip, and pocketed it. But by-and-large the anglers would use the bins provided. Quite why anyone would put loaves of bread, half-used cans of luncheon meat or tubs of cheese paste in the bins in the first place I never understood. Surely they knew it would rot, smell and attract vermin?

As the years progressed the oil drums gradually rusted away, and as the base collapsed, so their capacity would diminish, up to a point where they were of little use other than as a mouse house or rat flat. Waste would fall out of the many holes in the sides, while the wind would blow the contents off the top and spread it across the bank-side. Eventually the bins were of so little use I took them away over a period of a year or so. I had every intention of replacing them, and meantime expected to have to pay for their absence with more regular litter picks, but to my amazement, I found that there was no increase in litter; in fact, there was actually a reduction, as there was no wind-spread litter to collect. I'm pleased to say that ultimately I ended up with no litter bins on any of my waters, and virtually no litter – what a result!

When Ant and Dec Came To Stay

Our youngest daughter Emma was learning to play the violin, which was a struggle for anyone within earshot. The guests were remarkably tolerant, but her venture into catgut squealing did have one saving grace. Emma's music teacher, Dave Montgomery (a Coventry City fan, but we can forgive him for that under the circumstances), was kind and tolerant with her efforts. He was also involved in an education-based music and arts programme that sought to bring popular music to the children of Scotland though the schools system. Dave noticed a Geordie duo that would fit the bill perfectly, if he could just persuade them to attend. At just this time the up and coming 'Ant and Dec' were trying to break into the music scene having become famous on kids TV though the programme *Byker Grove*. They retained their character names of 'PJ and Duncan' for their music act, and enjoyed some considerable success in the UK charts. Who could possibly forget *Let's Get Ready to Rumble?* I know I cannot, try as I might.

Dave also knew the owner of a local guest house who was a fellow Geordie, someone who would undoubtedly offer them a warm welcome with comfortable accommodation – namely wor lass, Jackie, at The Palakona Guest House. I'm not saying that the prospect of a visit to our establishment was the driving force behind the boys deciding to come to Newton Stewart, but you never know.

Sadly, I missed this momentous occasion as I had a fishing trip to Eire arranged and couldn't reasonably back out at such a late stage. But I did try to experience part of the occasion and share in the excitement via phone calls from a phone box in Portumna. It wasn't easy, but I felt it was the least I could do.

Apparently, all went well; the two lads were pleasant, down to earth, amusing and friendly. Jackie cooked them a meal of braising-steak, having learnt that this was Ant's favourite.

The local girls all went into hysterical fan mode, one of them fainting outside our door as the stars came downstairs before being hurried into a waiting car. My eldest daughter, Adele, had managed to blag a seat in the car too, much to the chagrin of her sister Emma who has yet to forgive her to this day.

By all reports, PJ and Duncan went down a storm at the local nightclub, 'The Riverside'. I'm reliably informed by those present that it was packed, hot, sweaty and loud, just as such an event should be. Teenage hormones formed an almost visible curtain in the air, mixing with the heady aroma of 'Exclamation,' a scent that seemed to be all pervasive for the girls, while the fellers were drenched in Lynx 'Africa'. Little wonder the hole in the ozone layer was causing concern, was it, lads?

Adele and a young 'Ant' aka 'PJ' 1994.

The session finished relatively early in the evening as PJ and Duncan were heading off to London in the early hours of the following morning. They chilled out in the lounge of the Palakona, chatting with Jackie, Adele and Emma. Their manager enjoyed a can of beer, while the boys gorged themselves on tea and Jaffa cakes, not very rock and roll. The boys were kept busy signing autographs that Adele had been given strict orders to obtain for a long list of school pals.

They were up and away very early in the morning as promised, leaving my girls free to ransack their room for mementos, having arisen uncommonly early for a school-day. Apparently, Adele made a killing at school the next day, selling autographs, used blocks of soap, pillow cases and even cigarette ends!

Back To The Day Job

The tourist season of 1994 proved to be a busy time for us, thank goodness. All aspects of the business were beginning to pick up and demonstrate their potential. The fishery commitments were onerous. Bailiffing and weed clearance were very time consuming, the latter being physically draining, too – oh, how my back ached.

The direct correlation between weather conditions and sport was driven home with depressing force this summer, too.

Diary Entry, August, 1994:
Two Pike anglers switched their attentions to carp and enjoyed themselves at Craichlaw. They caught a mirror of 7lb-8oz and four tench to 4lb 12oz, all on hair rigged birdseed boilies.
Overall cooler weather led to poor sport, few tench coming to the net but plenty of silver fish and perch, a highlight being one perch of 1lb 10oz.
I do feel a sense of hopelessness. Craichlaw has been emptied and de-silted, I've weed-killed it, fed it with lime and manure and I've spent thousands of pounds re-stocking it and still it fishes badly!
Yet again we've had a cool summer with temperatures rarely above 18c. It is only scant consolation to learn that other local waters are fishing badly too.
Cold blustery showers all day. We even had ½ inch of hailstones today.

Occasionally, I would take it upon myself to try fishing venues further afield, partly in an effort to maintain my faith in fishing per-se. It could become so tiresome fishing the same waters, but also to try different techniques. I had fished Loch Ken so frequently throughout the 1980's that the fish and I exchanged Christmas cards. In addition, I found on the odd occasion that I did go to fish Loch Ken that I was plagued by pests – Signal Crayfish being one, and anglers from Wigan being another. I'm not sure which were the bigger nuisance.

Ireland was one place I enjoyed venturing to, but this involved an expensive ferry trip so I opted to try somewhere more local.

I spent an overnighter on the Castle Loch at Loch Maben, just over an hour's drive away, where I applied Irish bream fishing techniques. I sought local advice, thereby establishing the best swims and bait. I located the shelf, where the shallows gave way to deeper water, albeit a long way out! I fed heavily with groundbait over the edge of the shelf, before setting up camp for the night.

I needn't have bothered with my camp-bed and bivvy. I was hardly in it all night. I landed 95lb of prime Scottish bream, the largest being 7lb 12oz, and all of which were taken on red maggot, worm or both. I've never been so happy to have had a disturbed night's sleep. I just wish one more fish had obliged, to help me hit the magic century mark.

Thank goodness I remembered to take my camera. But what a shame the batteries were dead. There weren't any solar powered battery chargers available in those days, or cameras in your phone. Few of my angling 'friends' believed me on my return, and I reckon they still don't.

Diary Entry, October 1994:
This weekend I went pike fishing on Loch Dee with the renowned Terry Knight from Burton Mere Fishery and Richard Leigh of the Angling Times. This reconnoitre was for the forthcoming pike competition to be held there next week. Richard and I never had a run all day but Terry had one at 18lb 6oz and another at 12lb 4oz, both taken from off the jetty. Local chap, John Thomas had one at 9lb 8oz too.
Terry demonstrated how to use inflated balloons and paper clips to guide your bait to its intended location, very clever and a technique I used regularly thereafter

until I realised the environmental damage I would be causing.

Terry Knight, Loch Dee 18lb 6oz.

Diary entry, November 1994:
Loch Dee competition was a complete fiasco! Poorly organised, I'm pleased I was frozen out of the arrangements and promotion by the FC (Forestry Commission) now! Disgruntled anglers can't blame me this time.
Torrential rain didn't help but really, amateurs at work who didn't understand what they had taken on. 140 pike anglers over two days and on a prime trout water, rarely fished for pike and only six pike were caught in total! The best fish was only 10lb 4oz. Myself, my friends and my guests were all soaked to the skin for little reward.

Loch Dee is a beautifully located prime trout loch, set in the midst of the stunning Galloway countryside. As well as being a trout fishery, it was used at the time as a place to bring on farmed trout for sale. This meant good vehicular access, so long as you had a key for the gates! Although the water could be somewhat acidic, the loch held excellent stocks of trout, and consequently a healthy population of protein fed pike. Rumours of 30lb-plus pike being captured on a regular basis in fyke nets were commonplace.

Part of the fish-farming business saw two large cages sited just off a lengthy jetty that projected out into the water. On the few occasions that I was able to fish Loch Dee it was in the immediate vicinity of these cages that I found the pike. I reasoned that they were drawn there by the proximity and activity of the enclosed trout, but also by the attraction of feeding on both escapees and the resident wild trout, themselves drawn to the cages by spilled feed.

As a beautiful, relaxing pike venue it was all you could ask for . . . except that pike fishing was only permitted two days a year and it was fyke netted on a regular basis, with all pike captured thus immediately killed.

The pike competition was arranged by the FC as an experiment for potential future commercial exploitation of the water. Sadly the entire event was an utter fiasco, from promotion, accommodation, car-parking, bait supplies, rules, registration and weigh stations, right through to the awards ceremony, publicity and press reports. For me personally, it merely confirmed my worst fears regarding the incompatibility of pike fishing and competitions.

1994 drew to an end with unseasonably warm weather. We enjoyed an Indian summer throughout October with temperatures still in the high teens. The fishing responded accordingly with carp, tench, roach and bream all showing from our waters. Even by late November we had temperatures of 11c-14c when Kev landed a 3lb13 oz tench from peg one at Craichlaw.

Elsewhere in 1994...

The usual dip in visitor numbers occurred as we approached the end of the year. This was not good economically, but it gave Jackie and me time to draw breath. If only we could have afforded a holiday. Of course, our friends and family considered us to be enjoying one long holiday.

It was very easy to become safely ensconced within our bubble of life. We were aware of the rest of the world and what was happening, we watched the news and read the newspapers but somehow it seemed to be in a separate galaxy, far, far away, where 'others' lived but not us.

In 1994:

A huge earthquake hit Los Angeles.

Ayrton Senna was killed a Grand Prix car crash.

Nelson Mandela became South Africa's first ever black president.

Labour chose Tony Blair as its leader.

Sunday trading in the UK was legalised.

The IRA declared a 'complete' ceasefire.

Norway voted 'No' to the EU.

The UK's first lottery took place.

The last event on this particular list did awaken me from my bubble somewhat, as it led to me meeting Bob Nudd, the four-time World Angling Champion and fishing legend here in yickle old Newton Stewart. He and his wife were heading to Northern Ireland, where Bob was due to compete in an international fishing competition. His wife had insisted that they stop to purchase a lottery ticket, as there was no guarantee of a lottery ticket outlet where they were heading. As I recall, this was the first ever UK National Lottery draw.

I noticed his sponsored car parked outside the local Co-op and couldn't resist introducing myself and having a chat. It was fortuitous, too, as Kev and I were going to the very same spot that Bob was fishing, just a few days later – Portglenone, on the River Bann. Bob kindly suggested that I look out for him.

On our eventual arrival I made a beeline for Bob along the riverbank. I did my usual trick of distraction. He missed bites, as I pumped him for tips and advice. He was tolerant, kind and courteous. He didn't mind my interrogation too much, telling me that he'd conceded the match anyway, and advised me the best place to fish was "past the ski-jump". He did warn me that it had been hard work, though; the bream just hadn't shown up to the party.

He was right. Kev and I enjoyed a relaxing few days, but catches were poor, even by our lowly standards.

Back home our regular rough shooters, inland wild-fowlers and the occasional pike angler saw the guest house tick over. We had now become accustomed to 20 per cent winter occupancy, and no longer panicked about it. However, this was to be the last winter that we had to rely solely on income from our various business arms to make ends meet. 1995 was to be a pivotal year for us all.

10 1995: A YEAR OF CHANGE

It was good to welcome so many familiar faces back, as the shooting season opened up again. It really was like meeting up with old friends. We would sit in the lounge and updated one another about what had happened over the previous year. This would include the usual stuff, such as job changes, additions to families, and changes in relationships, but it would also be when we heard why certain group members were absent, which would sometimes sadly be because they had passed away.

This would be our fourth winter accommodating guests from the shooting fraternity, and I was becoming more accustomed to the wildfowlers' unique ways. I no longer found it strange to hear them loading up their pick-ups at 5:00 a.m. on a bleak, freezing cold winter's morning to go out and lie in the estuarial mud. *Each to their own,* I would muse, as I packed up my car with pike gear an hour later to go and break the ice on a nearby loch. I was inured to the sight of geese, pheasants, decapitated deer heads or rabbits hanging from the rafters in the outhouse. Even my kids barely gave such gruesome scenes a passing glance.

A combination of shooters, passing trade and visiting pike anglers sustained us through the back end of '94 and into the early part of '95. However, I could sense in the wind that our lives were going to change.

The tackle and bait shop was very quiet through the winter months.

We would sell a fair amount of frozen pike baits to local anglers, and sometimes groups of sea anglers would unexpectedly arrive. They'd flood the shop, expecting to purchase rag/lug worm or razor-fish in large numbers, but without having pre-ordered these they would often unfortunately leave disappointed, cursing at whoever in their group had forgotten to do the job.

Usually, though, the shop was quiet throughout the winter. We could often go for days with no customers whatsoever. Such periods would give me a chance to spring clean. Moving large freezer cabinets and fridges around was no easy matter, while removing out-of-date frozen baits was cold on the fingers and harsh on the accounts – 'stock losses' were considerable.

Palakona Bait Supplies: bait storage room.

I was facing a dilemma on the fishery front. Having given up any involvement in the caravan park water, I was looking for another challenge and another water to add to the portfolio that 'Craichlaw Fisheries' possessed. Yet at the same time I'd agreed with Jackie to gradually wind down the fishery activity levels.

Diary Entry, January 1995:
Recent weeks have seen cold, wintry conditions with
poor catches as a result.
An otter has returned and taken a 4-5lb carp from
Glendarroch plus a few smaller fish but strangely
nothing from Craichlaw although spraint is evident
around the boat-house.
Should I go for Barnbarroch Loch? I'd love to and it's a
real challenge but, oh the costs and the work involved!
Meanwhile I've plenty to do at Whitefield Loch, our
latest pike water.

Whitefield Loch

Whitefield Loch is a fairly large water of some 60 acres or so, nearer to Glenluce than Newton Stewart; I negotiated a lease there, hoping it might prove to be the big water I felt we needed to add to our portfolio. Rodney Goodship was the proprietor of a nearby pub, The Cock Inn, and was also a shooting enthusiast. He leased a long stretch of the bank-side from a local farmer to shoot duck and geese on a commercial basis. Rodney and I formed an informal partnership to use the loch for both shooting and pike fishing. The Forestry Commission had a stretch of the bank-side, too, as did a local angling club, leaving the remainder to Rodney and me.

The water contained some lovely perch over 2lb and some roach, too. Time proved that the pike weren't large. Any capture near 20lb was a rare event, but at least the Loch did provide good sport for smaller pike. This meant that I could safely send guests there, secure in the knowledge that that they would almost certainly catch a few pike, albeit in the range of 4lb to 12lb, rather than monsters. Experience subsequently showed that the large perch were as popular as the pike. The lure of those elusive 3lb specimens drew many perch anglers, and some came agonisingly close to achieving their goal, alas without success. A perch of 2lb 12oz was recorded by one our guests, while a superb specimen of 4lb 2oz was caught during explorative netting exercises just a few months previously.

A number of factors led to me dissociating Craichlaw Fisheries from a loch with such wonderful potential. One of these factors was that I was offered 16 pike, varying in weight from 8lb to 20lb and all netted from the protein-rich trout water the 'Lake of Monteith' in Perthshire. These were being sold at a bargain price of 80p per pound, with the buyer to collect. Sadly, Rodney wasn't keen and refused my offer to go 50/50 on the cost. Ironically, these particular fish did end up with us in Galloway, as I contacted the fishery manager for Loch Heron and Loch Ronald, Jim Stewart, to tip him off. Jim knew a bargain when he saw one, and promptly concluded the deal. He went up to collect them and they were duly stocked in Ronald and Heron.

Despite the fact it drained directly into the sea, I was refused permission to stock Whitefield Loch with any other species of coarse fish; it would have made a perfect bream water in my opinion. This, too, was very disappointing.

After a year or so, I found that travelling the significant distance for maintenance, litter picking, and bailiffing, and resolving constant disputes over shared boundaries, all proved just too much, so I reluctantly declined the opportunity to enter into negotiations to renew the lease.

Whitefield Loch remains a popular venue for pike competitions amongst the local pike enthusiasts. But it still doesn't have a reputation for large pike. If only the authorities had allowed me to stock with bream and roach all those years ago as I had requested, and if I'd only been able to introduce a new line of bigger fish into the existing pike gene pool through the Lake of Monteith fish, I'm confident that 25-30lb pike would now be commonplace.

Barnbarroch Loch

Ever since I had been exploring Galloway as a holidaymaker, and enjoying the fishing it offered throughout the 1980's, I had been captivated by a nearby water called 'Barnbarroch Loch' at Whauphill, just a few miles out of Newton Stewart. It was another shallow and weedy water of seven acres, with a maximum depth of eight feet; it held a good head of tench, originally transferred from Craichlaw Loch decades before, and also bream, rudd, roach/bream hybrids, eels and perch. A previous leaseholder (also from Wigan, by a strange coincidence) had put a few carp in, many years ago too.

It was a quiet and secluded spot, hidden away in a small wood. When fishing it as a holiday maker I was rarely disturbed by other anglers, and I enjoyed catching decent bream up to 4lb that fought more like rudd (I was convinced they were hybrids). As is common in local waters, eels were a constant presence, and grew to a fair size of 2-3lb.

In January 1995, I learned that the lease was to become available. I turned over the question of whether I should apply for it.

The positive points were:
i)   Here was an already established, if dormant, coarse fishing water with a previous known record and reputation of catches and stock.
ii) This would be a replacement for the lost caravan park water.
iii) The acquisition of Barnbarroch Loch would send out a statement that Craichlaw Fisheries was continuing to thrive and expand.

The negative points were:
i)   Yet more financial investment was required, some £250 p.a. for the fishing and shooting rights alone. Then there were the considerable costs of stocking carp . . .
ii) A huge amount of work was needed to rebuild jetties, bridges, fishing platforms and to cut swims through the dense weed beds.
iii) All our previous advertising literature would need amending and updating at some considerable cost
iv) It would be yet another water requiring bailiffing.

In truth, my applying for the lease was never really in doubt. I was so excited at the prospect that I rationalised away the negatives and made a formal bid to the local Forestry Commission (FC) who owned the land and the water.

I was duly summoned for an interview and was offered the lease at the bid-price, but with some conditions that I hadn't considered. These conditions were:

1) I had to keep the very long perimeter fence in good order.

2) I was required to keep vermin and other wildlife levels in check, including deer. I was to submit an annual record of all kills.

3) The lease was only to run initially for three years.

As I sat in the office at the FC, rapidly debating in my mind whether I could meet all these conditions, I realised that I needed time to consider. So, a whole 30 seconds later we shook hands and I signed the forms. Well, I figured, how hard could it be to repair a few strands of barbed wire fencing? Kev and our winter guests would be delighted to keep the unwelcome wildlife numbers down, and as for the short tenure of lease? Perhaps that wouldn't be a bad thing, after my experience with the caravan park owner.

Barnbarroch Loch, 1995.

Ongoing Thoughts

Back on guest house duties, and the spring of 1995 saw a gradual increase in visitors for accommodation, but also customers in the bait and tackle shop.

We enjoyed – and for the most part, 'enjoyed' *is* the appropriate word – the company of complete strangers. Looked at objectively, the very nature of a guest house or B&B is a strange affair, running utterly contrary to the established notion of 'an Englishman's home is his castle'. In essence, the proprietors and guests are involved in a mutually beneficial trade-off that involves an invasion of privacy in return for financial recompense. We were no different. We offered accommodation in our house and home in return for money. At its very basic level it was as mercenary as that! But in order to thrive and survive in that relationship, we had to offer something different. Something that was perhaps indefinable, possibly even inexplicable, yet highly valued.

On reflection, our success didn't come down to any one quintessential factor, but rather as a result of a combination of factors. We catered to our market, which was outdoor pursuits, in a very practical way. We provided a drying room, a bait fridge, kennels, and a gun safe. We offered a bait and tackle shop, private fishing and shooting, with local knowledge. There was a public phone for guests to use, which was important before the days of widespread mobile phone ownership. We provided off-street private parking. We were also close to the town facilities of shops, pubs, restaurants, the Tourist Information Centre and the River Cree (which was important for our salmon anglers). Our guests were given keys and trusted to come and go as they wished, without unduly disturbing us or our neighbours. (The latter wasn't always managed!)

Jackie would cook delicious meals of well-prepared, traditional fayre, but would also have alternatives on the menu where requested. We were happy to offer meals at very flexible times on an 'as and when needed' basis. Packed lunches were available; indeed we even offered packed breakfasts. And did I mention that we were cheap? £13 p.p., per night, an absolute snip.

The bedrooms were comfortable, warm and double-glazed with a TV and alarm clock radios. Jackie was constantly decorating. There was adequate wardrobe space, and although we didn't have en-suite bedrooms we did have shower and toilet facilities on each floor.

The lounge had a dart board, two open fires, comfortable settees and a large TV. We even offered a CD player, which represented a state of the art music system at the time!

Lounge and dining room, Palakona Guest House.

We didn't feel there was any one magic ingredient that created a successful tourist business. It was more of a formula or recipe, a carefully managed mixture of various factors that came together to create the necessary prerequisite for success. As proprietors we tried to be friendly, affable and understanding of people's needs. A sense of humour and a great degree of tolerance was required, helping to form the foundation for a happy relationship with our customers . . . usually!

Our previous occupations in the field of mental health certainly gave us the interactional skills required to foster the kind of relationships needed. We recognised that our guests were often very much out of their comfort zone. They were strangers in a town where in most cases they knew absolutely no one. Some came in familiar groups, but for others, like salesmen or solo tradesmen, it could be a lonely existence.

It was not unheard of for us to have to deal with wet beds or 'body odour' (BO) issues. One solo guest had such a pungent BO problem that our other guests vacated the dining room in disgust when he entered, insisting that I speak to him before they'd contemplate a return! I did speak to him; I had to, because Jackie adamantly refused! I think he suspected why I'd asked to have a chat with him when he saw the gas-mask I was wearing as I entered his room. The poor chap was acutely embarrassed. His explanation for the odour was rather vague, and seemed to be the result of a somewhat dark recent history involving the police, prison, social services, living rough, and a stay in hospital. Thankfully, having a shower and sending his rancid smelling clothes to the nearby laundromat did the trick.

Wetting the bed, meanwhile, was uncommon, but not unheard of. We levied a standing charge of £25 for a mattress replacement. We would approach the person concerned discreetly, and tried to deal with it politely. If the guilty person refused to pay up, we found that the prospect of his mates finding out was usually enough to make him change his mind. And yes, it was always a 'him'.

On another occasion we had a middle-aged father and his 11 year-old son staying with us. For reasons undisclosed and not pursued, Dad told us that they needed some quality time together, "A time for bonding," as he put it. The pair would spend the entire day fishing, taking a packed lunch with them. On their return, they would enjoy an evening meal either with us or at the local chip shop or take-away. All seemed to be going well, and there was a noticeable warming in their relationship toward each other as the days progressed. Until one morning   .   .   .

The incident in question must have happened on the fourth day of their stay. The lad came down for breakfast in tears, refusing to speak. He wouldn't explain why he was so upset. At first, I suspected perhaps he'd wet the bed – it wouldn't have been the first time I'd had to raise such a sensitive issue. When Dad had gone back upstairs, I had a few words with the lad in the privacy of the empty lounge and asked if he'd had an accident that he was embarrassed about? The poor lad was aghast at the very suggestion. He was so annoyed that on his Dad's return he revealed all.

Apparently, his father snored so badly that it kept the boy awake all night. He knew that this trip was of the utmost importance to his Dad, and didn't want to spoil things by complaining, so he had kept quiet and cat-napped while fishing to catch-up on his sleep. In an effort to try to improve matters he decided to roll up small pieces of newspaper, stuffing them in his ears in an attempt to form a crude set of earplugs. Sadly, this didn't help with the noise reduction, so he upped the paper level each night. However, he didn't recognise the crucial need to remove the previous nights' inserts. By the time he revealed his secret to me, his ears were blocked and painful. I had a look using a torch; it wasn't a pretty sight. Both ears were inflamed with a seeping brown/yellow discharge; it was no wonder the poor lad was in such pain. I phoned the local hospital, where the on-call doctor agreed to examine him. The doctor used forceps to remove the various pieces of newspaper. As a fellow angler, he was quite amused to discover that the cause of the fishing trip misery was a selection of small, rolled-up extracts from The Angling Times.

Eardrops were prescribed, earplugs purchased from the local chemist, and all was well. The lad even caught his first ever carp later that evening. Happy days all round.

Heatwave and sadness

Dumfries and Galloway enjoyed a warm and, for the most part, sunny summer in 1995. As a result, the fishing improved, although the various waters remained frustratingly inconsistent.

On a personal level, tragic news reached me from out there in the 'real' world. On June 14th I was greatly upset to learn that one of my greatest musical heroes had died. Rory Gallagher played the guitar like no guitarist I had heard before, or since. He enabled blues/rock to have real meaning to me, while his lyrics touched a nerve deep in my soul. During a difficult and lonely period of my life as a young man it was Rory Gallagher that helped me through; I owed him much. He died in a London hospital at the tragically young age of just 47, due to complications following a liver transplant. RIP Rory and thank you, your music lives on . . .

Also during that summer

Blackburn Rovers won the English Premier League, while Rangers won the Scottish League for the seventh year on the spin and Celtic won the Scottish Cup. Astonishingly, Raith Rovers had won the Scottish League Cup, beating Celtic in the final.

Everton won the English FA Cup, while Frank Bruno won the WBC Heavyweight belt. The mighty Wigan Athletic were bought by multi-millionaire Dave Whelan and began their dizzy rise to the top, despite only finishing 14th in the English league division three that season.

John Major won a Conservative Party leadership battle. The movie *Braveheart* was released, and in news that may perhaps have been related to this, the 'Deep Fried Mars Bar' was apparently released upon the world, in Stonehaven, Scotland, thus capping a wonderful year.

Diary Entries June/July/August 1995:
June: PHEW WHAT A SCORCHER! The hot spell

continues, tench have finally stopped spawning. I've been watching them closely from up the tree, I suspect there are actually only a few breeding females.

We've had a power cut and for some reason I awoke at 6:00 a.m. almost sensing problems. I rushed out to the shop and sure enough there were maggots everywhere. Thankfully the power can't have been off too long as the freezer units and contents remain frozen. I had to lift the carpets and move all the units to sweep and vacuum the maggots up.

As I write it is 7:00 a.m. and the electricity supply has just come back on. The temperature is already 18c despite a blustery Nth East wind, for which we are grateful, temperatures of 26c are expected today.

July: The searing heat gave way to more manageable conditions. It's been close and muggy 22c with many thunderstorms and power cuts.

Craichlaw remains frustratingly inconsistent; some lads enjoy themselves while others blank. Glendarroch and Barnbarroch are both producing plenty of bits but Culscadden is worryingly low. What is going on? The water level is about 3 foot down but still producing a fish a cast.

August: It's been a long hot summer! These shallow, wee lochans don't have much water in them to start with. With the exception of Craichlaw all my own waters are as low as I have ever seen them. But . . . they are all producing good sport with tench, roach, rudd, perch and bream all showing regularly.

I even found crucian carp while I was cutting weeds in Barnbarroch and Glendarroch.

The significant volume of water loss from three of my most productive waters was worrying. I was selling day-tickets to anglers who had to wade out into thick, oozing mud to set up. The fish also had to adapt to low oxygen levels, gathering in increasingly large shoals in ever reducing areas of water.

Gradually I was able to establish just what was contributing to the problem. Obviously the unusually hot and sustained weather was one factor. This had real consequences for Culscadden, where the surrounding farm found many of its usual natural springs had run dry. Cattle needed watering, and the contents of the farm pond were the next obvious point of water supply. A tractor would frequently appear and fill a large water bowser from the waterside. I'd seen this before, of course, during times of normal water levels, and even in winter – but during drought conditions I worried for the welfare of the fish, in the immediate term, and for the long term future of the water as a fishing venue. The pond was rapidly ebbing away in front of my eyes. Only three pegs could be used.

Barnbarroch Loch is a burn-fed loch, and as the burn dried up, so did the loch. At least it had slightly more depth to sustain the health of the fish population than Culscadden. Nevertheless, some of the pegs became utterly inaccessible, with the fishing platforms marooned in a sea of mud.

Glendarroch Loch was also burn-fed, by a burn that was now dry. The loch had drained down to an even more worrying degree, eventually consisting of just one small pool of water in the corner just three feet deep. But the dry weather conditions turned out not to be the only cause of the rapid water loss. I discovered that water was draining away through a leak in the outlet culvert to the overflow pipe. I never found out exactly what had caused the tear, but it took Kev and I a lot of hard work to put things right. Our efforts were worthwhile, as the repair remains sound to this day, nearly 30 years later!

Troublesome Neighbours

The tackle shop owner who, in my opinion, had been wilfully refusing to acknowledge the existence of Craichlaw Fisheries for some time now, really began to show his true colours at this time. I'd tried to maintain cordial relations with him, while admittedly at the same time encroaching upon his 'patch'. He found himself an ally in the form of an elderly local couple who had moved into the house a couple of doors up from us. One small window to the rear of their house looked out toward our tackle shop. We didn't mind the intrusion, but they weren't happy with the shop at all. This seemed strange, given that they owned their own shop down the street. The two parties joined forces and launched a campaign of attrition in an effort to have our bait and tackle shop closed down.

It was all rather immature; at no point did they actually come and speak to us or even confront us. The new resident would park his car across the archway, thus preventing access to our car park, annoying us and our guests, but also our neighbour Eric, who was an on-call fireman and missed a number of call-outs as a result.

They actually sank to name calling! We were "Incoming White Settlers," and they would shout at us to "go back home" whenever they saw us, before dashing into the house and slamming the front door behind them before we could respond! It felt like we were back at school in the playground.

On one occasion, they made a formal complaint to the local Community Council regarding an advertising sign we had placed on the pavement against our wall at the front of the guest house, directing customers down the alleyway to the shop. Their complaint was a ploy that backfired badly, though, because it led to ALL businesses in the town having to remove any and all advertising signs, including products on display that encroached on to the pavement. Understandably, the complainants became rather unpopular with many of the other shopkeepers in the town as a result.

One day they upped the ante still further. I noticed a local tradesman working on their back roof, installing a downspout from the guttering. The next time we had heavy rain, the water gushed from the downspout and through a strategically placed plastic culvert, emptying directly up against our shop frontage and creating a pool of muddy water that customers had to negotiate. It was clear that this would lead to potential long-term damp issues in the masonry if not resolved.

A word with our solicitor led us to understand that under Scottish law, homeowners were indeed entitled to direct rainwater from off their property and if necessary, onto their neighbour's land. Of course, the same law meant that we could do likewise. So we did. We introduced a drain to take rainwater through a pipe that went beneath the shop floor and out of the back wall, gushing down onto the neighbour's garden below. I must admit that I did feel a bit foolish engaging in such childish games, but the drainage problem needed solving and it felt satisfying to get one over on them.

Another element of this strange and childish campaign came to light when we received a letter purporting to come from a so called 'director' of 'House of Hardy', the world-renowned fishing tackle manufacturer, claiming that we were in breach of copyright by using the name 'Palakona'. House of Hardy manufactured a very famous salmon rod made from Palakona, a Spanish cane, and had branded the rod with the same name. Again, a brief search and a legal bill of £82.80 established that we had nothing to worry about. I discovered later that one of the so called 'legal advisors' involved was a shooting friend of the tackle shop owner.

The bait and tackle shop did require formal planning permission, however. Despite it having previously served as both a barbers shop and a newspaper shop, a 'change of use' order was required. We were granted a three-year temporary consent, and despite an objection (submitted by guess who?), permanent planning permission was duly granted the following year.

'Prestigious' bait shop is given go-ahead

WHAT has been described as the "most prestigious bait shop" between the west coast and Carlisle has been given permanent planning consent.

Mr K. Barlow has been operating the tackle and bait shop at 30A Queen Street, Newton Stewart, on a three-year temporary consent to see how it affected the surrounding area.

There was just one objection submitted, from Mr and Mrs ██████ 34 Queen Street, but when the application was considered last week by Mid Galloway local area committee, Mr Peter Matthews, for the couple, said conditions imposed on the development would meet most of their points.

Remaining was the matter of road safety. It was clear there would be problems with delivery lorries using the pend from Queen Street to the business. If they drove in they would have to reverse out.

But, Mr John Axtell, 32 Queen Street, said he had never seen any commercial vehicles go into the pend, which was owned by him.

A report to the committee by the planning department pointed out that no complaints about the shop had been received during the temporary consent, apart from one relating to a sign on the pavement. W.F.P. 2|11|96

Interior of the Bait and Tackle Shop, and a report of the planning permission granted.

I should point out that this piece of nonsense was one of very few disagreements we ever experienced with local people. By far the vast majority were, and still remain, friendly, welcoming and generous in their approach to us incoming, white English settlers!

There's one exception to this, of course. If ever there's a football or rugby game taking place between the two countries, things are not quite so friendly. Scottish folk support two teams – Scotland, and anyone playing England at anything!

When 'Big Jack' Called In For Breakfast

One Sunday morning, I was busy serving breakfast to a squad of coarse anglers from Glasgow when the doorbell rang. We were full, the 'No Vacancies' sign was showing, and the tackle shop was closed, so I was a bit miffed to have to answer the door while serving hot meals to 12 hungry anglers.

I got a surprise when I did answer the door and was confronted by a famous footballer! It was 1966 World Cup winner, ex-Footballer of The Year, one time manager of Middlesbrough, Sheffield Wednesday and Newcastle United and at the time, very successful manager of the Irish International team, 'Big Jack' Charlton, who asked if we could possibly rustle up breakfast for him and his family.

"Of course we can!" I stuttered, somewhat star-struck, and then went to check with Jackie if we indeed did have enough ingredients to actually do so! Thankfully, we did.

Jack duly returned with his wife, Pat and two granddaughters. He explained that he was driving to Ireland to continue his Irish FA manager duties, when a deer had leapt out in front of the car causing a minor bump. There appeared to be no major damage to either party (the deer ran off into the woods), but Jack wanted the car checking out before proceeding any further. Jack had been a long-time visitor to Newton Stewart when fishing the River Cree for salmon so he knew the area well, and used his contacts to find a mechanic to inspect the car. He had even stayed at The Palakona Guest House on a number of occasions in previous years, leading him to bring his family to join us for breakfast.

Jack Charlton was an accomplished salmon angler of some repute, and it wasn't long before banter ensued between the Glaswegian coarse anglers and the Geordie salmon angler. "In God's name, why would a Scotsman take up coarse fishing?" he asked, incredulously. "The same way an Englishman gets to manage the Irish Football team," was the instant response from one of the Glasgow boys! A game of convivial and light-hearted verbal tennis ensued throughout the time together only brought to an end by the lads going off to "drown some more maggots," as Jack suggested.

I couldn't resist bringing up the time when the then lowly non-league, Wigan Athletic beat his Sheffield Wednesday team in the FA Cup some years ago. He was strangely reticent about the topic, claiming to have only just taken over at Hillsborough at the time and having a poor memory of the game itself. He said this with a knowing wink!

Eventually his car was given the all-clear and delivered to the door, whereupon Jack's wife Pat took the grandkids to prepare to continue their journey. While they were out of sight Jack came through to the back yard where he begged a sneaky fag from Jackie and me. He told us how he was under strict doctor's orders to stop smoking, and his wife was monitoring this very diligently, having confiscated his packet of cigarettes. He also borrowed some breath mints to take with him.

I can't for the life of me think why I didn't ask Jack to sign the visitor's book. He was an approachable, quick witted and good-humoured man, whose passing recently at the age of 85 due to dementia was very sad indeed. I can just imagine him as he arrived at The Pearly Gates saying to St Peter "Now listen, bonny lad, if there's nay fishing up here I ain't coming in."

A Fisherman's Friend

Alan Hedley enjoyed his fishing; he didn't always enjoy purchasing a day-ticket or joining the local Angling Association, though. Nor did he always use his rod and line to catch his fish, if you know what I mean.

However one evening he was fishing legally on the River Cree with his friend and angling rival, Barry. It was getting dark when Alan latched into a huge sea-trout. Estimating it to be a personal best (PB), they both agreed it was bigger than Barry's PB, too, which was far more important. With his pal watching on and sniggering loudly, somehow Alan contrived to lose the fish. He cursed his luck, and sloped way into the darkness to have a drink from his hipflask and to lick his wounds, well out of earshot of the taunts of his pal.

A few minutes later, he heard a lot of splashing further up the river, and there, just visible in the beam of his night light, was a large dog otter, wrestling with an enormous Sea Trout in its jaws. Alan chased after it and managed to startle the otter into dropping its prize conveniently on the bank-side, thereby enabling him to claim it for his own. Alan immediately ran down the riverbank in search of his mate, triumphantly holding his prize and claiming bragging rights, while not disclosing exactly how he had 'caught' the fish. The sea-trout weighed in at a little over 11lb and was duly accepted as a superb specimen, while also setting the bar higher in the PB stakes between the two rivals.

There are a few post-scripts to this Tartan Tale.

Choosing his moment carefully, quite some time later, Alan revealed the truth to Barry. I believe friendly verbal punches were exchanged, and that he has yet to be forgiven.

Alan received £22 from the nearby Crown Hotel for his catch.

At that time Alan and I used to frequent the same pub, The MacMillan Inn, about which a separate book could be written. A few days after the otter incident, Alan enjoyed a few drinks too many, as was – and sadly still is – his want. He left the pub, and I chased after him as he staggered up the street to tell him that he had left his rod and tackle behind.

"Och I'll no need that stuff nae more Kenny, I'll just get my trained otter to catch ma fish noo," replied Alan.

KEN BARLOW

11 THE MACMILLAN INN

Ahh!! The blue fug of fag smoke and the equally blue language, the political incorrectness and the warmth of the welcome; it all comes flooding back. On being greeted by, "Evening Kenny, you Wigan c**t!" I'd reply with, "Good evening, Mick, and how are you?" His usual response to this was, "What are you, my fakkin' doctor now?"

Mick Barker and The MacMillan Inn was a unique pub experience and believe you me, I've been in a few over the past very many years.

Mick had owned a coal merchant business for many years and had also been a postman, both "darn sarf". He was a talented footballer, playing for Barnet FC at one point. Mick had served in the army doing his National Service, which involved serving during the Mau-Mau uprising in Kenya.

Mick and Bet Barker bought The Mac on a whim after Mick saw a tiny advert in the Exchange and Mart for a pub for sale in Scotland. The pub in question, The MacMillan Inn, turned out to be not much bigger than the advert. They fell in love with the pub, and the town of Newton Stewart. For Mick it realised a long-held dream to become the landlord of his own pub.

The family moved in 1985 from Colchester, buying The Mac from Iris Rigg. With the help of his family and local tradesman Rob McDonald, who was the main builder, they refurbished the whole place. So much work needed doing that it was February 1986 before Bet and Mick were able, with the help of sons Pete and Tim, to open the doors to become mine hosts. As they say, the rest is history.

Mick and Bet, re-opening of The MacMillan Inn, 1986

Mick insisted that there would be no dartboard, jukebox or TV, which was just as well really, as there was little room for any of those. But dominoes, cards, banter, earnest debate and camaraderie flourished. At night, it was a lively place where discourse varied from politics to football, jokes to anecdotes and more gossip than the wash-hoose. Mick enjoyed and encouraged board games. One of these games was called 'Shut the Box'. I never really understood it, but I know that it involved a lot of shouting and swearing, especially if Mick was losing.

There was a radio behind the bar, strictly for personal use and definitely NOT for public entertainment of course, because that would need a licence. If Mick was bored or he heard a favourite song come on the radio, he would suddenly raise the volume to maximum level, causing all conversation to cease, or go to shouting level. Once he'd had his fun Mick would abruptly turn it back down again. This ploy would leave people shouting at each other, occasionally revealing intimate conversation to the entire pub!

Thankfully Bet was always on hand to intervene when necessary, for example, when it was half an hour after closing time and Mick was still serving freely.

One year we had convinced a rather drunken Mick that it was New Year's Eve, and he kindly stayed open late to let us see in the New Year, as he usually did. It was actually December 30th. Bet came bouncing into the bar, admonishing us all and throwing us out. It took Mick a few days to forgive us.

The Mac was a place where the restrictions of 'normal' human discourse could be set aside, particularly if you were a regular. Take Clive, for instance, who would serenade you with his unique baritone rendition of Happy Birthday; it mattered not a jot that it wasn't your birthday, nor that he could barely hold a note. Or old Jimmy, who, in return for a wee dram, would spout forth the poem 'Twa Crows'. Even the locals needed a translator to understand his version.

It was also a place where 'The Gurk' would sit at the end of the bar and whack you with his walking stick for no apparent reason. Mick and Tim always ensured that the Gurk got a taxi home with his Kit-Kat bar and a cigar, no matter what state he was in. Until one evening, when the poor chap didn't make it home. He died in the taxi, reportedly still waving his walking stick in defiance of the grim reaper.

Mick had a caring side that he did his best to hide. He and Bet would always ensure that if any of their regulars found themselves in need, they were cared for. A warm meal would be provided, if necessary. He would visit folk in hospital or at home if they were ill. He or Bet would collect prescriptions and/or food, and deliver them to the door. Mick would also drive folk to visit friends or family in hospital, sometimes as far away as Dumfries – a round trip of 120 miles. I would sometimes hear of his kindness, but if I mentioned it to him he would swear me to secrecy. "I don't want every cant finding out Kenny, for faks' sake; they'll all want f'kin help, won't they?"

One regular, Vic, found himself homeless and sleeping in the cab of a lorry (or worse). Mick and Bet took pity on him, and offered him temporary lodgings until he could sort himself out. Knowing a good thing when he saw one, Vic saw no reason to reject this act of kindness, nor indeed to rush his decision making regarding his future. He was still a 'temporary' guest two years later.

The pub's swear box was actually a large whisky bottle, and it sat proudly on the bar. As you can imagine by now, the swear box would fill very quickly in The Mac. In truth it became largely reserved for holidaymakers, or non-regulars who over-stepped the mark. It was fine for us regulars (especially the bar staff!) to swear like troopers, but if an incomer did so a sudden silence would descend, and a finger would be pointed to the swear bottle. Only on the payment of a hefty 'fine' would the noisy conversation resume. Mick would empty the contents on a regular basis, and donate it to the local Day Centre.

We would send our guests to The Mac, but with a very clear word of warning as to what to expect! Mick wasn't a keen angler at all. "Wot's fishing? I'll tell ya . . . a rod with a hook on one end and silly cant at the other," was his definition of anyone who went fishing. (With due apologies to Samuel Johnson.)

On one occasion, we had a group of lads from Liverpool staying with us. One night and midst heavy drinking, the group leader fell foul of Mick's acerbic manner and vicious wit, and they fell out. The exchange of insults and barbed witticisms was wondrous to behold for the rest of us, consisting of Scouse humour versus Cockney humour being batted back and forth for an hour or so; superb entertainment. Sadly, it all went a bit too far and the visiting angler stormed out of the pub, shouting, cursing and beating his chest like an angry gorilla. He flounced out, fully expecting his pals to follow him, but they didn't, being all too busy trying to control their tears of laughter.

A few minutes later the same chap, realising that his roommate had the guest house door key, sneaked back in trying to avoid being seen by Mick. Of course he was spotted immediately, and Mick launched into him.

"Oi . . . wot you after? Lost your f'kin teddy bear, 'ave ya? Frightened to walk home in the dark on yer own, are ya?"

The poor chap just had to take it on the chin and slink back out, key in hand.

The next day Mick called in to the guest house and had a chat with the hungover chap concerned, they shook hands, and the same fellow became a regular at The Mac for the rest of that trip and many other subsequent visits. For those of us anticipating more heated verbal exchanges it was all rather disappointing.

By day The Mac served almost as a day centre itself for a few of the local old folk. Some of these could make a pint last for two hours as they basked in the warmth of the coal fire, secure amongst friends.

I didn't enjoy many daytime sessions in the Mac, I was usually at work spinning plates. But on the occasions I did venture forth, I found it almost like a different pub entirely. It was dark, as usual, there being only one small window, and usually fairly quiet, too, with a few hardened old fellers enjoying putting the world to rights through rose-tinted spectacles. They did have some wonderful tales to tell! Spending time in their company taught me an important lesson for my subsequent work with people with dementia. These people may be old, curmudgeonly, and positively grumpy at times, but they had lived rich and interesting lives. These were people with a past littered equally with achievements and disappointments. They had experienced great sadness and utter joy. Just like people with dementia, they deserved the respect afforded them as people, not patients.

Joy and Sorrow

I was in The Mac one day, raising a drink to the memory of one of the old regulars who had passed away and to whose funeral some of us had been earlier in the day. The subdued conversation turned to grief, pain and the anguish of loss, when another old fixture at the bar, Chic, began his tale.

It was the mid-1950s, and Chic was ten years old. He had pestered his parents to let him have a puppy for many months. Dad was away serving in the Army, and only came home for occasional weekends, thus leaving all such major decisions to his wife. Chic's Mum was adamant that she was not having a puppy around the house. "Who'll be clearing up the mess and getting up in the night? Who'll end up taking it for walks when the novelty wears off? Then there are fleas, vets fees, dog food . . . NO!" This was her firm and oft repeated response.

Dad, however, was more open to the idea in principle, and Chic did what he could to get him onside with the idea. As his 11th birthday approached, Chic upped the pressure, and a couple of days beforehand a message arrived, instructing him to be at the local railway station for the 6:00 a.m. 'Paddy train', the regular rail service between Scotland and Ireland, on the morning of his birthday, to collect a very special present. He was not to be late.

Chic enlisted the help of his friend Davy, and, filled with excitement and anticipation, they awoke to a warm summer's dawn, and made their way up to Newton Stewart railway station. As the train whistled to announce its impending arrival and smoke appeared in the near distance, Chic did a little dance of delight on the station platform. He could barely contain himself at the thought that perhaps, just perhaps, his Dad had won the argument and he was about to become the owner of a wee puppy dog.

At this point in the telling of the tale Chic coughed politely, complained of a dry throat, and drew attention to his empty whisky glass. I duly obliged with the first refill of many, as the tale gradually unfurled. Apparently telling such grief-ridden tales was thirsty work.

The passengers all alighted and various boxes were thrown out of the guard's van, when suddenly a piercing whistle sounded and Chic heard his name being announced. A brown wooden box with air-holes drilled in the side was very gently placed on the platform, and the guard told Chic that this was a very special package for a special wee boy whose birthday it was today. He could barely control himself, as his shaking hands opened up the box to reveal a warm, black snout and fluffy ears. It was indeed a gorgeous puppy, and a puppy that was desperate to get out of its confines, scrambling to escape! The porter realised that potential disaster was imminent and quickly found some bailing twine to make a temporary lead, that he placed around the pup's neck. The pup was delighted to taste fresh air, and licked and kissed Chic and Davy with slobbery gratitude.

Chic recalled tears of joy pouring down his face as the guard explained that the present came with a message from his Dad, wishing him a happy birthday but also instructing him that he was to look after the dog and not to expect his Mum to do so. 'Oh, and leave your Mum's wrath to me,' the message said.

Chic and Davy set off down the road, with the puppy jumping and burling around, chewing on the twine and pulling hard to get free. Chic decided that he would demonstrate his good intentions and earn some much-needed Brownie points by taking the dog for a long walk before taking it home. There, he would face the undoubted anger of his Mum, before putting the dog in the shed and obediently going off to school. At least, that was the plan.

They entered the wide-open fields of his youth, and deciding that there was no further danger from traffic, they unleashed the pup and watched him leap and frolic with sheer puppy exuberance in the long grass down by the river. They chased after him, playing hide and seek, and both shrieking with giddy laughter as the puppy raced away in ever increasing circles.

"And that, Kenny boy, was the last we ever saw of the wee shite . . ." muttered Chic, abruptly! "He was way too good at the hiding. I didnae have him long enough to even give him a name," he added, ruefully.

He explained how he and Davy searched the fields for hours, their vision spoiled by blurred and teary eyes before going home and raising the alarm. They both skived off school for the next few days to visit nearby farms as they continued their forlorn search. They organised search parties and put up 'puppy lost' posters around the town, all to no avail.

Such was the intense sense of loss and grief that Chic experienced, he never, ever had another pet. "Not so much as a hamster," he said, explaining that he didn't want to experience that level of emotional pain again.

He was clearly still very upset by the memory all these years later, and needed a number of whiskies to recover his poise. On the day he told his tale I don't know whose anguish was the greater. Chic had a tear in his eye, certainly. But so did I. That tale of woe cost me a small fortune.

More Shedding Tears

It is fair to say that Rab – another regular – enjoyed a good drink. He tended to be an early evening drinker, before going home for a bite to eat. However, he began to overdo things and incurred the wrath of his wife, Jeannie, who found herself frequently having to go and find him or 'sort him out' on his eventual return home. In exasperation, she came to an arrangement with the bar staff at The Mac. They would only serve him an agreed amount, and they would order him a taxi in time to have him home by 9:00 p.m. each evening. This worked quite well for a few months, although Rab found the alcohol rationing very annoying. He worked as a labourer with the local council, and was rarely off sick; indeed he was never off work due to alcohol-related illness. He was rarely late for work, and often volunteered for overtime, so he reasoned that his drink allowance should be increased if anything, not reduced. Jeannie did not agree!

Rab came to his own agreement with The Mac bar staff: he would comply with the original agreement reached, but would take a few cans of Tennent's Extra Strong Lager home as a carry-out. These he would secretly hide in his garden shed before entering the house. He would reassure Jeannie that all was well, at which point she would retire to bed leaving Rab free to "Potter about in the shed," as he would put it.

Again, this worked well until one day . . .

The local council were replacing all the doors on the council houses, and Rab was involved in the process. He noticed that the old doors, which were all of different colours and hues, were thrown into a skip for disposal. Now, Rab's garden shed was dilapidated in the extreme, and he figured that the old doors would make ideal replacements for the shed walls. He was given permission to take as many as he needed, in what was probably one of the earliest examples of recycling undertaken by the local council.

Rab took the external back doors, with no letter boxes or windows. One Saturday morning, he removed all the existing shed walls and gradually replaced them with the new doors. He was pleased with the results, which were solid, waterproof and more importantly, all absolutely free. He even had enough spare doors to replace the leaking roof, ready for felting. He had worked up a fierce thirst with his labours, it having been a warm sunny day.

Jeannie returned from work and headed straight out to inspect the new shed. She was aghast! Here in her pristine back garden was a multi coloured monstrosity of a construction, the like of which she had never seen before in her life. "Looks like something off a kids TV programme, get it sorted!" she shrieked. She was as furious as she was embarrassed. Fearing what the neighbours would think, she insisted that Rab at the very least paint the entire thing . . . now!

Rab managed to locate some green paint going free, and set-to hurriedly painting the entire shed. It took him all afternoon to complete the task. By this stage in proceedings he was very, very thirsty indeed, and leaving the paint to dry he went to The MacMillan Inn for a well-deserved drink or two.

Rab persuaded Tim and Mick that because of his hard work today he had earned special dispensation to have 'a couple' more drinks than usual, and he did! As per the agreed arrangement, albeit a little later than usual, Rab piled out of the taxi at home with his carry-out in hand. He went to the shed to hide his secret stash, as usual. To his horror, he found an entire shed of doors! Exactly which of the plethora of identical doors granted him access was a secret that his drunken mind refused to comprehend.

The paint was still tacky, but dry enough to have sealed the door closed tight. In his efforts to force entry via the numerous doors on offer to him, Rab smeared himself in paint. Worst of all, his swearing and banging had stirred Jeannie to come outside to see what the fuss was all about. She discovered a frustrated and furious Rab, smeared in green paint. He was red-faced, staggering about as he carefully clutched his secret carry-out, while at the same time trying to hide its very existence from Jeannie.

Jeannie realised what had happened, and figured out that it obviously must have been happening for months. She was furious. She forced him to take off his paint-stained jacket and boots before entering the house. She then used a handy umbrella to prod him upstairs "like a coo at the market" as Rab put it when telling his tale later. She forced him into his bed before returning to the shed, where, in what was surely an act of sheer vengeance, she pierced holes in the no longer secret cans of lager with the umbrella tip.

The next day Jeannie went to have a few choice words with The MacMillan bar-staff. Mick and Tim both denied all knowledge of any carry-out, insisting that Rab must have stopped on the way home to buy this from the off-licence. She wasn't convinced, and thereafter poor Rab was made to use a different pub closer to home, and one over whose bar-staff Jeannie had more influence, along with speedier access.

But what of the shed? I hear you ask. Well, the door that was actually a door eventually became apparent in the cool light of day (and sobriety). The guilty party was found to have sealed itself shut because of the copious amounts of paint Rab had lavished upon it in his haste to get the job finished and him off to the pub. This explained its refusal to open on that fateful night, although not fitting the handle hadn't helped, either. He sorted the problem out by forcing the door open, sanding down the paint and adding a handle. The shed stood proudly for many years, as did Rab and Jeannie.

Mick the 'Hell's Angel'

Tam and Maggie McClelland (God rest her soul) were keen motorcycle enthusiasts, and both were active members of the local motorcycle club in Newton Stewart. They were also both regulars in The MacMillan Inn, where Mick regularly told them of the time when he too had been a 'Hell's Angel', back in the day.

Mick regaled them with vague but fascinating stories of an old and much-loved bike of his that he had 'chopped' into a customised machine of some standing. He had virtually mothballed this beast in his garage, only occasionally taking it out for a run.

One Sunday morning, Tam and Maggie had arranged a motorcycle club meet in Dashwood Square, immediately outside The Mac. They pleaded with Mick to bring his much revered and talked about bike, as everyone was keen to see the modifications he had introduced.

The bikers all lined up, revving their engines and admiring each other's bikes as they prepared for a blast up the coast, when Mick came racing around the corner. Resplendent in a black tasselled leather jacket, biker boots, a helmet, gauntlets, even sunglasses, he stood imperiously astride his Raleigh Chopper bicycle, circa 1973.

Farewell To The Mac

Whether through the day or at night, you needed a thick skin and to be of quick repost to survive The MacMillan experience. No prisoners were taken, and no quarter given. The repartee was wicked, funny and invariably entirely accurate.

With Roger away at sea, and Pete off to University in Nottingham, son number three, Tim, had long ago returned from Clacton on Sea to continue to support the family business. Tim had inherited his Dad's sense of humour and he became synonymous with the entire Mac experience. We became quite friendly. One weekend away saw me introducing Tim and his family to the wonders of the DW Stadium and various pubs in Wigan, while on a later occasion we also visited St James's Park and the pubs of Newcastle-upon-Tyne. Later in his short-lived life I visited him in York, where he and his lovely family had set up home. Tim's untimely death in 2014 was a massive blow to his family and all who knew him, especially me. I still miss him to this day.

Mick was prone to a rare medical condition, referred to by those who knew him as BIFS (Booze Induced Flu Syndrome). The older Mick got, the longer it took him to recover from his bouts of 'Flu'. Partly due to this, in 2005 he and Bet felt that the time was right to retire. The decision was greeted with dismay and abject despondency by the many regulars. Indeed, such was the devastation caused by this earth-shattering news that the local Samaritans phone line was busy for many weeks. The members of the various tribes of The MacMillan family became scattered, only bumping into one another on occasions in other pubs in town. The MacMillan Inn was converted back into a house where Mick and Bet enjoyed a quiet and contented retirement until sadly Mick passed away in March 2015. I'm pleased to say that Bet still lives there and thrives to this day.

Meanwhile, for as long as there are ex-regulars to tell the tales, the legacy of The MacMillan will live on. Some evenings, when I am parting from my wee boozing buddy Les on the corner of Princes Street immediately outside where The Mac used to be, I swear I can hear Mick through the open window passing comment on our conversation with his usual disdainful "Listen to 'em . . .fak'n 'opeless."

(Photo credited to Bert Malcolm)

12 WHERE TO FISH IN GALLOWAY

I had helped the local tourist board compile the coarse fishing details in their fishing guide brochures for three years. It came as an annoying surprise to discover that some unnamed 'desk jockey' had changed many of the details for the latest edition without even asking me to proofread it, as I had in previous years. There were many glaring mistakes that caused confusion and conflict regarding permit outlets, boundaries and even fishery/accommodation ownership. The Tourist Board refused to change the error-strewn guide for the following season; I resigned as a member in protest.

In conjunction with this, and somewhat annoyed by recent articles in the *Angling Times* that suggested the best coarse fishing in Scotland was to be found in the Central Belt, I found myself able to reply and rectify this view to a certain extent, through the magazine published by The Scottish Federation of Coarse Angling.

That article follows, and gives an accurate picture of the coarse fishing scene at the time in Galloway. It was subsequently posted on-line and apparently formed the basis for a guide for many years to come. It's out of date now, of course, but if you search on-line 'Coarse Fishing in Dumfries and Galloway', it often pops up, almost like a well-presented dead bait:

COARSE FISHING IN THE
SOUTH WEST of SCOTLAND

by Ken Barlow

Many of the coarse anglers in the central belt of Scotland seem to have forgotten that there is some excellent fishing to be had in the South West. **Ken Barlow,** *of the Palakona Guest House, knows the area very well and here takes us on a tour of the waters down his way . . .*

Despite the impression given by recent *Angling Times* articles, Coarse fishing in Scotland is not confined to the central region of Glasgow and Edinburgh. Many coarse anglers from England, Scotland and even abroad have learned over the years that for quality and choice there is really only one part of Scotland to head for – the south west!

Largely unaffected by industrial pollution and enjoying a mild climate, Dumfries and Galloway has proved to be a receptive region for the development of coarse fisheries, much to the chagrin, it has to be said, of many local game anglers. Geographically, the region has lent itself to influence from the north of England towns and cities just a short drive away for many years now. As far back as the 1950s, during the English close season, a trip to Loch Ken or the Castle Loch at Maben was within easy striking distance of the North West and North East conurbations. Then, as motorways were built and car ownership increased throughout the '60s and '70s, so it was that more and more visitors explored the attractions of South West Scotland, bringing their desire for coarse fishing with them. Some came and stayed to develop coarse fisheries to meet the needs of the aforementioned visitors. Others came, fished (often for pike), and returned home having tipped surplus live baits into whichever loch they had been fishing. This deplorable practise led to the spread of coarse fish throughout the region, but at the same time set up the bad feeling which exists today between the game and coarse fishing fraternities.

The factors briefly mentioned above may well explain the development of coarse fisheries and the concurrent stocking of non-native species in south west Scotland but there is one intriguing exception.

Thriving Tench

For some reason, and this region is not alone in this regard, there are waters in which tench have thrived since a time well before any influences of coarse anglers. With the exception of the usual pike, perch and eels, I can think of no other coarse species which can be said to indigenous to the still waters of Dumfries and Galloway. Scottish tench may not grow to the size of their English and Irish counterparts, but they lack none of their fighting abilities. They have adapted well to increased levels of acidified water and seem to spawn far more successfully than, say, bream or carp. I've even heard of them showing in large numbers in areas as far north and east as Dundee.

Now, I have a theory as to how tench were able to establish themselves and survive the effects of the usual culling to extermination by game anglers. The landed Victorians went through a mid-19th century period when it was all the rage to landscape the gardens of the estate and to include, in the manner of Capability Brown, ornamental gardens including fish ponds. One possibility is that tench were stocked into these waters as a deliberate policy to help in keep these estate lakes clean. Well known as bottom feeders, it may be that the Victorians included tench in their waters not for sport or beauty but rather for purely functional purposes, falsely believing that in scavenging amongst the bottom silt the Tench were 'purifying' the water for their beloved trout.

As we know, tench can tolerate very low levels of diffused oxygen. They prosper in neglected muddy pools, which any self-respecting game angler would treat with contempt. This being the case they would not be perceived as a threat to trout or salmon stocks and would largely be ignored in their silty abodes. It is well established that sometimes neglect and mother nature combine to create an ideal environment for fish to thrive. One indicator that my theory may have some validity is that three of the four waters in Dumfries and Galloway which have been known to hold tench for as long as locals can recall are all private, man-made waters set in the grounds of private estates.

As I indicated in the introduction, there are a large number of coarse waters in the region, (although only a limited amount of river coarse fishing); the interests of brevity mean that I cannot cover all of them in this particular piece. I will therefore concentrate on the waters I know particularly well. These lie in the west of the region, generally within a 20-mile radius of Newton Stewart.

CRAICHLAW FISHERIES

Consisting of five coarse waters, winter river fishing for pike and a brown trout pool, Craichlaw Fisheries operates from the Palakona Guest House/ Bait Supplies in Newton Stewart, where a bait and tackle shop also exists. (01671 40****). Guests and customers are offered accommodation, bait, tackle and permits, along with local knowledge, all on a one-stop basis. The waters are as follows:

Craichlaw Loch

Set in the grounds of a private estate, this Victorian creation has to be one of the most picturesque waters in Scotland, if not the UK. With a boat-house, oak-built bridges, an island, rhododendrons and banks of beautiful lilies, it looks the part, and, given the right conditions, can provide fabulous sport as well. Over the years there have been various stockings of carp, bream, crucians, roach, rudd and perch. But it is undoubtedly best-known for its tench fishing. Like most local waters, it has a tea-stain colour but is also very clear, and as a result, sunny weather can kill sport stone dead; even the roach and rudd seem to vanish. But fished dawn and dusk over a bed of hemp, corn and crumb, or on overcast but warm days, it can be a fish a chuck! The tench run to 7lb 2oz, (an unclaimed Scottish record at the time of writing) while a mirror carp of 26lb 9oz was caught five years ago. All baits score:

corn, maggot, boilies and bread; but I would advise anglers to avoid worms in the evening, unless you enjoy catching eels all night.

There are 28 dry-stone pegs, a car park, and toilets, and the site offers good access for disabled anglers. Day tickets must be purchased in advance from Palakona Bait Supply/Tackle shop (01671 40****), or as guests at the guest house.

Glendarroch Loch

Sister water to the above Craichlaw Loch and just across the road, Glendarroch is a shallow, gin clear, estate water holding a large head of roach, rudd and perch. Tench, carp and some bream have been introduced over the years to provide variety.

Again, low levels of light are the key to success on this water. If you must fish it on clear, sunny days, fish at a distance hard up to the lily and weed beds. Use only a little groundbait, and concentrate on the deeper (approximately 5ft) swims on the far side. However, once the summer sun goes down, expect action from the superbly marked rudd and the increasing number of tench, which currently go to about 3lb. There are 13 pegs, car parking, and reasonable access for disabled anglers. Day tickets as per Craichlaw Loch.

Culscadden Farm Pond

This tiny water holds some big surprises! Situated a couple of hundred yards from the sea it has a good head of roach, averaging ¾lb. The rudd are good quality, too, as are the perch, while the tench go to 3lb. It has been stocked with carp, crucian carp and a few bream in recent years. In addition, an as yet unidentified fish has been encountered frequently in recent years, but with no-one being able to land or even identify it! Some maintain it is merely a large eel, while others believe it to be a survivor from a stocking of 5 mirror carp introduced in 1988 at 7lb. Whatever it turns out to be, it is extremely crafty, never picking up bait on sturdy tackle, preferring to smash up fine lines instead! There are three comfortable roadside pegs and another four around the pond. Parking is available at the side of the loch. Day tickets, as for all Craichlaw Fisheries' Waters, must be purchased in advance from the Palakona Bait and Tackle shop, or as guests in the guest house.

Barnbarroch Loch

Once the premier water for coarse anglers in Wigtownshire, this loch had been sadly neglected for many years until Craichlaw Fisheries assumed the lease in March 1995. Since then a massive and surprisingly successful weed clearance programme has been undertaken. With new platforms and most of the loch re-opened to fishing, it is beginning to reveal some of its secrets, with rudd and bream both to 2lb having been landed so far. It is best known, however, as being a 'bits' water. For example, four anglers recently had 189 fish for 12lb! 12lb to 15lb bags are not uncommon to Matchmen who know their stuff.

Fine line techniques work best for the perch, hybrids roach and rudd. The pegs on the far side seem to be more consistent. Car parking is limited but reasonable, and 11 pegs have been reclaimed at the time of writing. Day tickets as for Craichlaw Loch, or from the nearby Whaup Hotel.

Whitefield Loch

This is a large pike loch of some 60 acres or so, and is well known for large perch. Craichlaw Fisheries are gradually introducing new species to offer greater diversity, but with such high levels of predation it is a long-term process. Perch to 2lb 12oz have been caught on rod and line this year, while a sample netting last year produced one of 4lb 2oz.

Usual ledgering tactics work well, but paternoster rigs also seem very effective. Very small sand eels and very large lobworms appear to work equally well, particularly fished at a long distance into deep water. Large plugs have accounted for excellent perch, recently.

This open loch is surrounded by mature mixed woodland, and with sudden ledges and drop-offs to 25ft, it is very reminiscent of many Irish loughs. If anyone has a few thousand bream to donate, just to complete the picture, we would be very grateful.

Day tickets again as for all Craichlaw Fisheries Waters, in advance from the Bait and Tackle shop or as guests. The Cock Inn at Auchenmalg also sells tickets.

River Bladnoch

This famous salmon river has certain beats open to pike and perch anglers through the winter months (November to March inclusive). A 21lb 6oz pike was landed recently, and returned, although mid-doubles are more frequently encountered. Ledgered dead baits seem quite effective, live baits and spinning is strictly forbidden. Large numbers of perch frequent the river, some of them reaching specimen size.

Anglers should always check availability before travelling. Tickets again from Palakona Bait Supplies in advance only.

CRAICHLAW FISHERIES ASSOCIATED WATERS . . .

Loch Heron

This is a water of some twenty-seven acres, and best known for its large head of pike. As coarse angling has flourished in Wigtownshire, so this water has been developed to retain popularity. There are 45 platformed pegs with good access. Pike to 26lb have been caught recently, and Craichlaw Fisheries have been influential in conjunction with the managers of the water, Galloway Country Sports, in a stocking programme that has seen pike between 12lb and 21lb introduced recently.

The main feed fish, and best alternative quarry, are roach, rudd and perch, with bream beginning to make themselves known. Some carp and tench have been introduced with a view to the future. Boat hire is available in advance, Day tickets in advance from Palakona or on bank.

Loch Ronald

A large water of some 100 acres plus, Ronald is immediately adjacent to Heron. It has a large head of indigenous roach, and there is also a fair quantity of good size trout. The pike are sometimes harder to locate than on Heron, but can be bigger. A favourite haunt is in the drop-off just in front of the boat slipway, although vaning or ballooning is often required to reach the exact spot. Boat hire available in advance, day tickets available as for Heron.

Monreith Loch

Also known as The White Loch of Myrton. Just beginning to flourish again after some serious incidents of farm pollution in the 1980s, Monreith has long had a justifiable reputation for pike fishing. Best in recent years is 21lb 8oz, while in late 1995 two guests claimed 42 Pike in three days, including 19 in one day. Only a few were doubles, but who cares! As the roach and rudd stocks slowly recover, so should the pike. Access for vehicles and car parking has been improved lately, while a country walk has recently been built, along with platforms for the disabled.

Not surprisingly, given the size of the natural prey, small silver baits are the best bait on this water: natural sprat, coarse fish, and/or silver barb, etc. Day tickets from Palakona as before or at Monreith House.

OTHER LOCAL WATERS

Spectacle Lochs

Two small but picturesque waters set in Penninghame Forest just outside Newton Stewart. Quite a well-known water, but often flatters to deceive. A large head of mainly small pike and good size perch are the main quarry. However, recent years have seen the capture in increasing numbers of roach, rudd and hybrids, some of them to 2½lbs. It can, however, be an infuriating water, in common with other local waters, because of its inconsistency. I once witnessed an angler take 64lb of roach and perch, while his mate fishing less than 15 yards away actually blanked!

Tench are present, but not in large numbers – if you get one, it will be a bonus. There is good access to the smaller of the two waters, where a picnic table and car park exists. A rather poorly located platform for disabled anglers also exists. This water is managed, just, by the Forestry Commission, and day tickets must be obtained from the keeper's cottage, Glenrazie Lodge, just down the road.

Garwackie Loch

This water is part of the same system as Spectacle and Eldrig. Garwackie is essentially a fun spot for some perch bashing or jack catching. As with Spectacle, a low double will be a good fish. Access is less easy than Spectacle, and I and our guests have enjoyed best pike sport off the cliff which indicates the drop-off. Day tickets as for Spectacle.

Loch Eldrig

The last of the Penninghame Forest lochs, and the one perhaps worst affected by high acid levels, there is nevertheless a fair head of pike here, with the best that I have heard of being 17lb 6oz. Access is down a long forestry track to car parking near the loch. Day tickets from Glenrazie Lodge again. Do note that the far bank of Eldrig is strictly private.

Torwood House Hotel

This country hotel located outside Glenluce has two coarse pools within the grounds, and Loch Dernagler for pike a few miles away. The pools in the grounds hold tench, roach, rudd, bream and carp. A tench of 6lb 14oz was landed recently. Access and car parking is good, day tickets available from reception.

Newton Farm Pond

A small lochan, situated within sight of the A75. This water holds large numbers of roach, rudd and perch, with some tench, progeny of Craichlaw, to provide interest. Pike are also present, some reaching 9lb. Access is across a small field from the farmhouse from which day tickets can be purchased.

Cairnhouse Farm and Drum Rae Lochs

Two small waters run by the local coarse angling association. These have been stocked heavily with a wide variety of fish, more with a view to the future than immediate gain. The weight gain of the carp suggests that we may not have too long to wait for success. Even the chub seem to have taken to the waters well. Membership is open to all on a yearly basis, but day tickets are only available for Drum Rae to regulars of good reputation. If coarse anglers have caravans in the area, it may be worth thinking about joining the association. For details, contact me as the secretary, details as above for Palakona Bait Supplies.

As I mentioned earlier, brevity is of the essence in this feature, and I have therefore excluded certain waters which it could be said are not coarse fisheries but rather are waters with coarse fish in them. Clatteringshaws and Loch Maberry are good examples of these.

Some Local Advice

Much of what follows applies everywhere in the UK, although I have tried to emphasise those things which are perhaps more important on local waters than elsewhere.

Many local waters are crystal clear, which, while having some obvious benefits, does also mean that in clear sunny/bright conditions, fishing can be very tricky indeed. This is particularly true when clarity is combined with shallow water so typical of many local waters. The use of canal black or similar can help, but in truth, if the day turns out to be clear, bright and sunny, the fishing is likely to be hard work! In such conditions, if you must fish daylight hours, as in a match, I would suggest that you head for a loch with deep water, or one that has a large head of fish such as Barnbarroch. In reality, however, fishing dawn and dusk on such days is essential, particularly if you are after carp, tench and bream.

I have never understood the inflexible approach adopted by visiting match anglers; they insist on fishing 10:00 a.m. to 4:00 p.m., come what may! Some of our regular match squads who are visiting on pleasure trips have learned to adapt to conditions and sometimes a 'split shift' match is arranged, whereby anglers fish from dawn to mid-morning, then head back in for breakfast, a quick nap, a visit to the bookies/pub/shops, etc, before returning to the venue for the second half of the match from, say, three hours before dark. I recall one such match being won with over 80lb of fish, mainly tench. I also recall a normal time match on the same water being won with 1lb 2oz!

If you are able to pre-feed a swim it is best to do so. No fish enjoy having crumb or corn, etc, showered down around their heads and into their gills. It is far better to have a carpet of bait in place for the fish to move on to. Guests of our guest house, and only our guests, can rake swims, under advice, on our waters, and this offers a tremendous advantage. Immediately upon finishing raking, scatter plenty of your proposed hook-baits in the swim and allow the sediment you've stirred up to settle back, lightly covering the free offerings. This appears more natural to the fish, and keeps them, particularly tench, in the swim much longer, as they root around finding the goodies.

I have a wide variety of baits available. There is nothing worse than finding the angler next to you bagging up on, say, mini-boilies, and these being the very bait you happen to have omitted from your list. Here, again, local advice can help in your preparations. Palakona Bait and Tackle shop has a good idea as to what baits are catching and where.

Do be quiet! I've seen swims emptied of carp in seconds by one clumsy angler dropping his tackle with a heavy thud. Similarly, quite how some anglers hope to catch fish while making the noise they do by shouting to one another is beyond me.

Come prepared for midges! They really can be an absolute menace and can ruin any angler's enjoyment. Find a midge repellent that suits your particular body chemistry, and make sure you bring it with you. We have also learned to use midge nets as added protection. The ones we stock are made by a local hill walker and are made of ultra-fine material, which keeps out all but the most determined midge.

Another word of advice: the shallow clear waters around these parts react quickly to temperature changes and rainfall. If the temperature remains in single figures, then forget good fishing; if it goes over 22°C, the same applies. However, if I'm confident of an overcast, drizzly day with a mild westerly and air temperatures around the 16°C to 18°C mark, I'll sit out all day on a pre-fed swim on virtually any of the waters here in Wigtownshire and district.

Finally, I hope that this article will help tempt you to try some of the waters of south west Scotland; contrary as they may sometimes be, they are well worth persevering with. For some readers it will be just a day trip, for others it will mean a weekend away, but hopefully for all anglers it will provide different angling experiences and new learning experiences.

Good Luck, and Tight Lines . . .

Ken Barlow

13 A TIME TO FISH AND A TIME TO PONDER

There is something utterly magical about sitting at the side of a beautiful estate lake such as Craichlaw Loch at dawn. With water lilies of various shades adding colour to the surface, and rhododendrons of different hues forming a natural backdrop, the setting is sublime. Add to this the swirling mist of early morning as it creeps upon the water, wreathing the lily pads, only slowly burning off as the sun rises to reveal the sheer beauty beneath, and this is nature at its most alluring. It is a calming, spiritual and enriching experience indeed.

The surprisingly noisy dawn chorus adds to the magic. Waterfowl chuckle and dibble across the water, sometimes starting in alarm at the unexpected and invasive presence of a well-camouflaged angler. Meanwhile, tench feeding bubbles fizz across the swim, carp crash and roll, while rudd dot the surface in playful abandon as they gleefully feed. It's not only that you feel appreciative of nature, you feel part *of* nature. There is a deep innate sense of belonging, of being at one with your surroundings. You, being there, at that time, in that moment . . . is nothing short of spiritual bliss.

I absolutely love tench fishing; they fight so hard and never give up fighting right up to the net. They are clever, too, being very aware of lily-pads, snags and other places of safety. They can be fickle feeders, sometimes hoovering up anything on offer, including the bait, while at other times they take anything but the bait!

I found that using the 'Lift Method' worked well on Craichlaw's silty bottom.

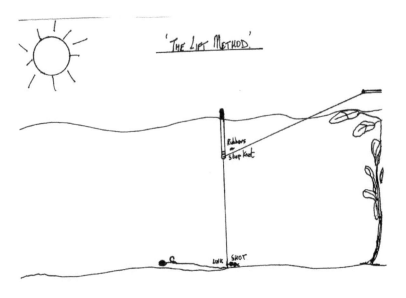

(The sketch I used to explain 'The Lift Method' to visiting anglers.)

Sometimes when the bait was taken the float would shoot up like a Polaris missile, while at other times it would be a minor tremor, followed by a slight rise then a gentle slide away into the depths. The Lift Method was less productive if there were many fish in the swim, whereupon the perpendicular line seemed to spook them, perhaps by brushing their fins as they fed with their heads down.

Usually, though, the technique produced exciting moments! Some sessions would see the tench feeding voraciously and I could land up to a dozen in a couple of hours, while other occasions would see me free to cogitate at leisure, only rarely finding my reveries disturbed by tiresome tasks like missing a bite or playing a fish. At times like this, mother-nature could see me as an observer rather than an active participant, and often left me to it. But because I was left free to ponder, less welcome thoughts would sometimes infiltrate my consciousness.

As the summer of 1995 began to turn to autumn, I knew I had

choices to make. This life was good for the soul in many ways, though stressful and demanding in others. My good friend Alan had sowed the seeds in my mind many months previously, by reminding me that I had responsibilities as a father and indeed as a husband and son. Of course, I was already aware of this, but Alan's reminder was timely and necessary because I kept putting it all to the back of my mind. Denial, rationalisation and other mental mechanisms were effectively protecting me from the tough decisions to be made.

One particular September morning, the customary glorious vista that lay in front of me as I soaked up another Craichlaw dawn seemed to try to seduce me into ignoring the decisions I had to make yet again. But deep down, I knew what I had to do. I had to pack up my fishing gear, go home and have my breakfast. Then I supposed I'd have to have the conversation with Jackie and the kids that I had been putting off for far too long. Change was undoubtedly coming.

When we had made the decision to change our lives so utterly five years previously, the agreed business plan, right from the off, included the condition that if necessary I would use my nursing background to procure full time employment. Was the time now right? Not essential, perhaps, but nonetheless necessary. My two daughters were performing reasonably well at school, and would certainly go on to make the grade for college or university. I knew that this would prove to be an expensive commitment. Further down the line, of course – hopefully *much* further – there would be two expensive weddings to pay for too, *yikes!*

Our current income levels were only just enough to get by; we were paying the bills but had nothing to spare after they were settled each month; we couldn't afford family holidays abroad, our car was old and nearer the scrap-yard than the showroom. Major improvements proposed to the guest house had brought in expensive quotes, while the price of fish stocks was soaring.

On top of this was the lifestyle, and the work-life balance issue. The very reason we moved in the first place was rearing its ugly head again, which was ironic, really. Jackie was finding the guest house increasingly trying and tedious, and she needed a change. As the number of waters in the fishery portfolio had expanded and the tackle shop thrived, so the demands on my time had increased, and it fell increasingly to Jackie to carry an extra load. We worked well together most of the time, but I would often be away bailiffing, weed clearing, checking out new waters, maintaining existing swims/platforms, dealing with shop salesmen, ordering stock and riddling maggots. This left Jackie with bedrooms to clean, laundry to launder, provisions to order, meals to prepare and cook, dishes to wash, bookings to take, a tackle shop to man and much more besides. Not to mention the demands of being a Mum to two teenaged daughters.

We had a chat.

The outcome was that I would set out to seek gainful employment. In addition, we agreed that we would try to not take bookings for such large numbers, with a view to eventually closing down the top floor of the guest house altogether. I would stop the fishery expansion, and reconsider the viability of the number of waters that I could reasonably manage.

Our two daughters were largely ambivalent towards it all. Adele was aged 15 and busy being a teenager, while Emma, 13 years old at the time, was deciding whether she was still a child or a youngster, the distinction was blurred.

So I set about reluctantly looking for work that I was suited for. I am inherently cautious to act. I'm a plodder; a tortoise rather than a hare, but I do persevere. I'm reluctant to give up on matters, and I seem to be good at handling 'people problems'. I knew I needed to choose my next move carefully.

I enlisted at the local job centre where I was repeatedly told that I was over-qualified for the various jobs that were available at the time. There were certainly no vacant mental health nurse posts in the area. I did apply for a job working with people with learning difficulties, and for one post at the local Social Services department as a Care Co-ordinator. I was unsuccessful on both counts, and most other applications were politely rejected or received no reply at all. I even made enquiries about nursing posts back on Tyneside from whence we started, though this would be very much a last resort.

I did find some part-time work using my teaching qualifications, offering lectures to the local Adult Education Service. These sessions were few and far between, and unfortunately the service eventually ceased to operate at a local level altogether – not because I'd become involved, I hasten to add.

Meanwhile with my various other hats on, life continued to provide all sorts of interesting experiences. I even found work cutting down Christmas Trees at one point – boy, that was hard work. The job involved cutting the trees down high up on the hills of the Galloway Forest, dragging them down the hillside, and forcing them through a netting machine, before finally stacking them on the back of a lorry, all in the middle of a downpour of steady and drenching rain. Not a career move for me, I was sure. No-one said my search would be easy . . .

DUMFRIES AND GALLOWAY COMMUNITY HEALTH NHS TRUST

R.M.N. 'E' GRADE

COMMUNITY PSYCHIATRIC NURSE
(2 POSTS)

1. Elderly/Adult based at Stranraer
2. Elderly based at Newton Stewart

Experience of working with the elderly mentally ill is desirable. Car owner/driver essential.

For further information contact Mrs Brenda Baird, Locality Nurse Manager, Tel. (01776) 702323.

Application form and job description from Department of Human Resources, High West, Crichton Hall, Crichton Royal Hospital, Dumfries (01387) 244427 to where completed applications should be returned by 3rd July, 1995.

Nursing Beckons

I had made the decision to seek full time employment in order to provide a more secure and less stressful future for my family. Then an advert appeared in the local newspaper. It advertised a job opportunity that I really could not ignore, even if I wanted to, which I didn't – at least that's what I kept telling myself. However, I did feel the need to have another sit down fishing session and a couple of lengthy dog walks to allow for a free-flowing internal dialogue of reflection to ensue to help me make the final decision.

If I successfully applied for one of these posts it would mean massive changes to the lifestyle we had created, and a return to the very chains of being a state employed wage slave, something I'd sought to escape from at the beginning of this entire adventure. It would also mean me having to shoehorn three jobs into one life. The guest house, the fishery/bait and tackle shop and now a full-time nursing post. Could I really plate spin like that?

On the other hand, it would see me return to a clinical, hands-on role of actually caring for people with significant mental health issues. This was a role I felt I had a natural inclination for, and one that I had a proven track-record of success in undertaking. In addition, the job would ease our financial worries and give reassurance and security for the future. The posts advertised were at a considerably lower grade than my last previous post as a Nurse Tutor, but I didn't mind that at all.

I discussed the situation with the carp and tench, who eventually gave their blessing to the idea, having ignored my bait. I also sought the advice of Digger the dog, whose barks of excitement during our walks of contemplation encouraged me to embrace the idea. I hurried home to tidy up my CV and complete the application forms.

The eventual interview with Brenda Baird, Angela Derry and co was tough. Really, really tough. Not one question was asked about fishing, shooting or riddling maggots. I think they must have been desperate to fill the posts, though, because I was offered the job and given a start date of September 1995.

14 FISHING HAT BACK ON

Diary Entry, October 1995:
Another Indian summer, just like last year,
temperatures remain relatively high, 18c today. Carp
and tench are feeding freely but at a distance at
Craichlaw.
Rain is gradually refilling the other waters although
critically low.
Plan for next year = 88 x 3lb carp from Framlingham
Fisheries.
Tony Taylor has been catching consistently all
summer, even when water levels were low.
Discuss water extraction issue with Culscadden Farmer.

A Different Kind of Deer (Stag) Stalking?

The guest house was usually quiet at this time of year as we awaited the shooters, but this particular October we were busy with passing trade. Anglers from Northern Ireland, the north of England and increasingly from the Central Belt of Scotland also arrived, looking for some fishing before winter set in.

Some of our guests purported to be anglers but weren't really! One such squad of lads all worked together, driving vans for a well-known chemical/medical supply company based in the Central Belt, distributing medical supplies all around Scotland. They were regular visitors and we got to know them quite well. They would book in ostensibly on a fishing trip but there were some weekends when what little fishing tackle they brought with them never saw the light of day, let alone the loch side!

On one occasion they booked in, stating in the phone call that they were coming for a 'stag do' as one of them had got married. When I queried this description of the order of events, I was assured that it was quite right. The Stag and his fiancé had arranged a spur of the moment wedding, leaving no time for a stag night. Not wishing to miss out, he'd arranged to have this *after* the wedding, here in Newton Stewart.

Late in the morning following the stag-do, I noticed our stag arrive in the dining room for breakfast and I went to take his order. I suggested that perhaps he'd prefer to wait for his mates to all to come down and join him. He muttered words to the effect of "You'll be lucky," but he went back upstairs anyway, only to immediately return and inform me that of the eight lads booked in, one was semi-comatose in his bed, while the other six wouldn't need breakfast as they hadn't come back from their night out!

The absentees eventually turned up in various states of dishevelment and at various times of the day. It transpired that they had all enjoyed a wonderful night out, leaving the local night-club in the early hours and being found accommodation by certain very welcoming local folk. One of them, with a big grin on his face, informed us that he wouldn't need his bed, or meals, all weekend. He did however seek our advice as to how best to remove visible evidence of love-bites.

"Fishing Can Be Heartbreaking . . ."

It was around this time that we had two brothers from Liverpool book in for a weekend away. They were regular guests, who enjoyed fly-fishing at Spa Wood Loch, our small but very productive trout water. Unfortunately, their stay was cut short when one of them started to feel unwell while out fishing. He sat down under a nearby tree for a sleep. His brother insisted on continuing to fish, happily catching brown trout and enjoying himself. His state of contented mindfulness was only broken by increasingly loud moans and gasps from his brother's direction. He told me how annoyed he was at having to reel in and trudge around the loch to see his "moaning minnie of a brother," as he later described him. It was only when he saw him profusely sweating, clutching his chest and drifting in and out of consciousness that he realised that he wasn't just suffering from a hangover, as he'd suspected. A quick trip to hospital confirmed he'd had a heart attack.

(Spa Wood Loch)

Many months later, the brothers booked in again. Following heart surgery, rehabilitation and on a mountain of medication, he felt that fishing would be highly therapeutic. "Just what I need," he'd said. His wife vehemently disagreed, and only very reluctantly allowed him to go fishing in Scotland, where apparently she envisaged wild, rugged, mountainous lochs in remote settings miles away from civilisation or medical care. She was so concerned that she repeatedly phoned us at the guest house, seeking reassurance. She had also equipped him with a state-of-the-art mobile phone, along with strict instructions for him to phone every hour. Meanwhile, the other brother had attended a first-aid course where CPR was taught and promised to never leave his brother's side while fishing.

The fishing didn't go well. "Every time he coughed or reached across his chest to his top pocket for a fly or scissors, I feared the worst. I'd drop my rod and run toward him." said the brother. Just as he was playing a particularly large and hard-fighting trout, his brother would playfully start moaning and complaining of chest pains! This trick didn't go down well.

I wish I could finish this Tartan Tale with a happy ending, but sadly I cannot. We learnt many months later that the brother with heart problems had suffered a massive heart attack, from which he didn't recover. He wasn't fishing at the time, nor was his brother with him; very sad.

Late autumn, 1995, gradually arrived in all its glory; it truly is beautiful in the Galloway Forest, where the different hues of gold, green and russet create a wondrous landscape. This year I noticed it all the more acutely, as I drove around the region in my newly acquired nursing role visiting patients and familiarising myself, through an induction programme, with the various resources available (or not, as the case may be), and the staff that operated them. The beauty of the landscape was sometimes in stark contrast to the many negative challenges that rurality and isolation brought about for people with mental health problems.

With my fishery/guest house hat on, I noted that, as usual, late autumn saw cooler temperatures set in, and we would see many of the carp and tench anglers being replaced by pike anglers. They were a keen, hardy bunch of angling specialists, whose enthusiasm would sometimes outweigh preparation and common sense!

Misguided or Misdirected?

Mark was a courteous young chap, and a real gentleman. He was a keen pike angler who always visited alone and travelled all the way from Crowborough in East Sussex. On this particular occasion he had journeyed through the night in order to create an extra day's fishing.

On a previous stay with us he'd heard good reports of Dernaglar Loch, and was keen to explore it as soon as possible. I had fished it just a few days previously, and enjoyed excellent sport. I'd landed no big monsters, but half a dozen pike up to 14lb with a much bigger fish slipping back into the water as I netted it. It also held large eels that were a nuisance in the evenings if you were after pike. The anglers Mark had previously spoken to had given him directions, plus bait and technique advice. I felt redundant; I also had job to get to. So after breakfast, Mark left excited and eager to fish, while I set off on the 25-mile commute to my office base in Stranraer.

We both met up that evening as Mark sat down for his evening meal. I was surprised to hear that he had blanked; indeed he had not had so much as a run all day. I suggested different techniques and baits that I'd found successful on that venue. For example, popped-up baits placed in the dying weeds had proved effective for me, as had adopting a roving approach, with the pike proving to be widespread around what was a sizeable piece of water.

Mark set off in the early morning gloom the following day to fish a dawn session. He came back for a mid-morning brunch. I was on a day off from work and thus was busy in the tackle shop when he came in to tell me, despondently, that he blanked yet again. I was puzzled; I drew him a map of likely spots to cover while he described the various swims he'd already tried. The two just did not marry up. The more he went into detail, the more I came to realise what had happened. Mark had taken direction from fellow pike anglers, who out of mischief or unpleasantness had not given the full picture. On the narrow rural track to reach Dernaglar Loch you had to pass a much smaller trout water, Barhapple Loch, which contained no or very few pike. (As a trout water it was regularly 'cleansed' of pike.) Mark's guides had made no mention of this first loch. He had followed the directions as given, came across what he presumed to be Dernaglar Loch, and set about fishing it. Little wonder the poor chap blanked.

He felt stupid and needed to restore his faith in himself and in the local pike waters, so he returned to a venue he knew well, The White

Loch of Myrton (Monreith Loch). Here, he landed a good number of small pike, as one almost always did there. It cheered him up no end, and the buoyant, bubbly Mark returned. He learnt a lesson about gleaning local information as a preparation for fishing: detail is everything. He also learnt 'The Six P's of Angling Preparation: 'Proper Planning Prevents Piss-Poor Performance.'

Readers will be relieved to hear that Mark returned to fish Dernaglar Loch on subsequent visits, and did indeed always catch pike.

(Success at last for Mark . . .)

Changes

We had established a cohort of regular return guests, who ensured that the panic of our early years in tenure was less evident. Nevertheless, learning to limit group numbers in light of my new job commitments was tricky. Sometimes I would walk through the back door to find Jackie frantically trying to meet the needs of eight or more hungry guests when someone – usually me, apparently – had messed up when taking the booking. On one occasion, I rushed to help with a group of shooters by serving the evening meals, not realising that I'd forgotten to remove my ID badge describing my role as 'Community Psychiatric Nurse'. This elicited various ribald comments regarding the mental well-being of some of those present. I couldn't, and didn't, argue, as far as many of them were concerned.

Having to work full time and also play my part in the guest house, tackle shop/bait supply and fishery business was proving to be a taxing adjustment process. Yet the differing nature of demands made upon me provided a strange but effective equilibrium. Being a Community Psychiatric Nurse in a rural area was stressful, of that there can be no doubt. I suspect that few of my colleagues would have found the idea of riddling maggots, cooking hemp or preserving caster a useful way to relax! I did, however. The shift in agendas, the thought processes and planning involved, and the complete role change were all positively therapeutic.

Furthermore, having a firm basis for financial security meant that we could afford a family holiday for the first time in seven years. It was a cheap, out of season, bargain break to Cyprus but very welcome indeed. The kids in particular enjoyed the change of environment and sunshine. To my surprise, I managed to locate some excellent carp fishing in a reservoir a few miles away. The Cypriot owner of a local taverna told me about it and kindly lent me his sea fishing gear. Fishing for carp with a beach-caster, 30lb line and sea hooks was an interesting exercise in adaptation. Competitive feeding amongst the many hungry carp meant that bite indicators were barely needed, if you let go of the rod you risked losing the fish and tackle altogether. It was great fun, but oh so very, very hot, with no shelter from the broiling overhead sun.

We returned home rejuvenated, but with those imponderable thoughts for the future unresolved and at the fore of our thinking, mine in particular. 1995 gradually came to an end, and as Christmas arrived, we found that the reputation the region had for a temperate climate did not preclude bouts of cold wintry weather.

A Cold and Snowy Winter; 1995/96

Diary Entry, December 1995:
Not much to report this past 2/12. Andrew has kindly agreed to forego the annual rent for Glendarroch Loch

to help with the costs of restocking due to the otter carnage.

Two of our guests caught 43 pike in 3 days fishing at Monreith Loch, 22 fish in one day, nothing very big but as one of them said . . ."with that amount of action . . . who cares?"

All of my waters have barely been fished so I've little to report. Neil has closed his aquarium at Skyreburn so I bought his coarse fish. I acquired 8 small carp including some crucians plus some rudd, roach, minnows and even a few sticklebacks. Most of these are for the fish-tank in the tackle shop, the rest for Glendarroch.

Christmas Eve – Today, Jackie and I stood in Dashwood Square singing carols as the snow fell all around us. It was wonderful! Our two girls were less impressed making a quick exit preferring the warmth of their bedrooms and their TV's.

29th – Since the last entry we have had no daytime temperature above freezing. 2 nights ago we had -12c. The fish tank in the shop froze solid, this despite it being indoors and with a pump left running. I gradually thawed out the contents and only lost two of the sticklebacks, verily 'twas a Christmas miracle! 2 inches of ice had formed on the surface of the carp tank in the garage, they survived too, just.

We have had no cold water on the top floor or in the kitchen of the guest house while there is NO running hot water whatsoever. The same is true of many other homes and businesses in town.

The River Cree and River Bladnoch are frozen solid with kids skating beneath the suspension bridge. It's all very Dickensian but very cold!

Finally . . . The sawmill failed to deliver the timber as promised so I cannot start work on building the walkway as planned on Peg One at Barnbarroch.

This cold snap was vicious, and lasted for five days. The timber for Barnbarroch Loch had actually been delivered, but was left half a mile away from the waterside, at the side of the main road. On learning of this, I had to go with a stinking hangover on New Year's Day to move it all to somewhere slightly less tempting for any passing scallywag. The following day I started to build one of the fishing platforms, but then decided to wait to judge the height of the water levels in the thaw before proceeding any further. At least, that was my excuse at the time.

The wildfowlers were determined not let a bit of snow prevent them from enjoying their sport. They travelled from England through snowfields, negotiating road conditions, contrary to police advice to come shooting for geese on the snow-bound, icy merse of Wigtown Bay. I'd long doubted their sanity. This merely confirmed matters.

(A Snow Goose; Winter 1996.)

The Joys of Rural Nursing

The photograph above was taken in the backyard of The Palakona Guest House in January 1996, and in the background is my car, partly hidden beneath a blanket of snow.

Such snowfalls invariably led to a warning from our nurse managers not to undertake routine visits that may put us at risk. On the day that photograph was taken, I couldn't get the car out of the yard and onto the main road, never mind undertake visits up rural roads and farm tracks. So I hoisted a shovel and a yard-brush over my shoulder, and walked down to the nearby Health Centre where my local sub-office was located. Here, I set about helping to clear the car park of snow, enabling the emergency services and on-call staff to operate more easily. For this, I was issued with a book token, many months later. Just how patronising can you get?

As the weather eased and temperatures rose slightly, I was able to return to my usual role as a Community Mental Health Nurse. The duties involved were varied and would include, amongst others, administering injections, undertaking mental health assessments, checking up on medication efficacy and side-effects, arranging hospital admission (or discharge), and of course offering ongoing, regular support and advice to patients and their families or carers.

To maintain therapeutic relationships with patients and relatives, frequent and reliable visits were important. With this in mind, as the worst of the snow thawed I phoned one of my patients to arrange a visit; her husband answered the phone. Things were not going well at home, he informed me, relieved that I would be calling. However, he warned me not to attempt to negotiate the farm track where they lived, as the snow was lingering; I should park up at the road end, instead, and he would come and meet me to give me a lift.

You can imagine my surprise and considerable boyhood excitement when he duly turned up in a big, shiny, red tractor! I clambered aboard, briefcase in hand, and spent the disappointingly short trip asking what each button meant, what handle did what and what all the dials on the instrument panel indicated. I was like a kid in the cabin of a jet plane.

On reaching the farmyard, I clambered gingerly backwards down the steps from the cab . . . and that was where the pleasure and excitement ended with a splash. I landed in a deep, smelly, cow-muck ridden puddle of icy cold slush. It went over my shoes and up to my ankles. The gentleman concerned asked me politely if I'd mind removing my shoes before entering the farmhouse.

We resolved most of the problems this couple were experiencing, but in truth the visit didn't last as long as I'd anticipated. It was a much more muted tractor trip back to my car. I returned to the Health Centre office where I draped my soggy, smelly socks over a radiator, much to the disquiet of my colleagues, I should add. Later, I had to bid farewell to my nice, new, and very comfy suede shoes. They never fully recovered. It took me a while to recover, too.

Diary Entry, February 1996:
When I wrote the previous diary entry I felt sure that the snow was near its end. Little did I realise that this latest snowfall would be even worse. It has snowed continuously for 33 hours! We have snow a foot deep in places, and much deeper where it has drifted. Helicopters are currently rescuing passengers from a train trapped in drifts at Barrhill. Many folk have no power, while none of us have had TV since Sunday night.
Many local shops have closed, there is no bread to be had, and none delivered. There is no post and no newspapers. Cars are stranded on the A75 near Annan and on the M74 at Lockerbie, both roads now closed.
I've done what I can at the Health Centre, answering messages, offering reassurance over the phone, as best as one can, phoning patients to arrange new appointments etc.
Finally I ventured out with Digger who was desperate for a walk having been trapped in all weekend. He loves the snow and frolics in it like a spring lamb. He also loves chasing after snowballs. I threw them upwards and he would leap to intercept them as they fell swallowing them whole. (He didn't find the yellow ones quite so tasty though.) Despite the chaos it has caused, the snow is indeed beautiful. We went out to Knockman's Wood where the snow glistened in the fields beneath the moonlight while above us in the trees crystallised branches formed a ceiling like a tunnel of ice. It was like walking through an ice cave.
As I write this it is 7-05pm and the snow has started

again, if only lightly. I do hope this doesn't damage my fish under the ice, how long before noxious gases build up, I wonder?

Throughout the next few weeks, we experienced further bouts of snow and ice. Digger and I went out in one of the snowstorms, and had to admit defeat after half an hour of battling against a sheer wind and icy particles that bit into my face. So fierce and unpleasant were conditions that evening that Digger even resorted to trying to walk backwards!

Work at Barnbarroch Loch came to standstill, partly due to the weather but also as I awaited news of a grant application for funding. Setting informed budget targets was a critical exercise, as I'd learnt painfully in the past. All the local waters were very quiet, but thankfully there was no sign of fish deaths from the conditions or as a result of otter predation.

During a short-lived mild spell I fished the far side of Barnbarroch Loch but blanked; quite an achievement on a water so full of fish. You can rely on me to fail in such situations.

Understandably, there wasn't much trade around for the guest house or the tackle shop. The shooters continued to visit but only in small numbers while passing trade was almost nil. Virtually no anglers came to stay, commercially times were bleak.

(Craichlaw Loch in her winter finery, beautiful to behold but impossible to fish.)

Diary Entry, March 1996:
Six rods fished Loch Dee. (I was playing football so
couldn't participate in a pike competition that was
part of an agreed pike removal programme.) Sunday
was mild in the midst of a cold spell and apparently
the big queens were in the shallows to the right of the
jetty. Final total was 12 fish, the best being 19lb 2oz
(by a strange coincidence there were two fish of
exactly this same weight.) No fish of less than 11lb and
all fish were successfully transferred to Loch Heron.

Football, after a fashion . . .

I had taken to playing football again in an effort to keep fit, but also because although I wasn't very good, I was keen, and I enjoyed playing, the latter usually helps in my experience. Quite a few of us were of a more mature age. I was 42 years old, for example, and while by no means being the oldest player, I was probably the slowest and least mobile, being a touch 'on the cuddly side'.

We played under the team name of 'The Pensioners', for obvious reasons, and competed on a Friday evening in the local 6-a-side courts but also in the local mid-week 6-a-side league. It was very popular and very competitive, with some rather tasty tackles going in at times too!

Occasionally 'The Pensioners' would form ourselves into an 11-a-side team and play against various local teams in friendly – or not so friendly – games. This was the case on the day of the Loch Dee pike match. The snow-covered pitch cut up very badly as the rain started. Skilful play was reduced to a minimum, the speed merchants found carrying the ball too tricky, and the slow, methodical cloggers like me came into our own. I had built my entire football 'career' (such as it was) on my ability to trundle around the pitch winning the ball. I would then pass it to another player – hopefully from my own team, though even this wasn't guaranteed – who could actually play a bit.

On this occasion, if my tackles didn't stop the opposing winger, the pitch would. It was all good, dirty fun. It took me a week to recover mind you. No weed cutting that week.

15 THE BEGINNING OF THE END

Spring of 1996 couldn't come soon enough, so we were relieved that by April we were enjoying warmer weather and slightly improved fishing.

Diary Entries, April 1996:

A Common carp was landed at Craichlaw today, 15lb 7oz from peg 9 caught on popped-up strawberry flavoured boilies. In superb condition apparently, taken by Gary Clarkson from Glasgow.

Meanwhile I've just about finished at Barnbarroch, I just need to await the rain filling it up to check if I've gauged the platform heights well or not.

Today I was cutting swims at Craichlaw, temp = 6-8c. Roach, rudd and perch all caught up in the weed I was pulling out, also lots of snails and caddis. This is exciting as it indicates my liming is helping improve the PH levels.

I'm convinced too that leaving the weeds alone throughout the autumn and winter helps mother nature manage the water quality. Of course it means I face an arduous task now cutting the swims! It's tedious and boring but has to be done and I suppose is strangely therapeutic.

Diary Entry, May 1996:
Here we are, well into May and there is still snow
visible up on the top of Cairnsmore, but no midges yet.
Cool northerly winds are keeping temperatures low, no
fish from my waters, nor anywhere else.

STOCKING.
Craichlaw . . .   76 carp @ 2lb to 15lb.
Barnbarroch . . . 10 carp @ 2lb plus 28 @ 8inch to 10
inch.
Glendarroch . . . 10 carp @ 2lb plus 26 @ 8 inch to
10 inch.

All in good condition but very hungry, within 24 hours
ten of them had been caught by day ticket anglers!
Most around the 2lb mark but one at 6lb 12oz to
Gary Clarkson."

(Ken and Jackie with two more carp for Craichlaw Loch.)

30th – These new carp have been most obliging
providing good if inconsistent sport. Total bags of 45lb
of mixed fish have been recorded. Red maggot, caster
and floaters have been best. Usually dawn and dusk
being best times.
Billy Halleran had a bream of 5lb 9oz which shows
excellent weight gain, (stocked in '94 at 4lb.)

> *Tench remain quiet and very few roach are showing at all. Weather remains cool and unsettled we've barely had 15c all spring.*

Of Midges and Men (and Women's hair do's)

This was the time of year when, as temperatures gradually increased, so Mother Nature stirred herself into full action mode. The weeds would grow as fast as I could cut them. I swear that as I pulled myself out of the muddy waters from which I'd just removed a ton of weeds, green shoots would emerge behind me.

I had honed my weed removal technique to a fine art by now. This involved wearing boots with steel toe-caps and appropriate clothing of either shorts and T-shirt or a dry/wet-suit, depending on the weather. I would carefully wade out, having set a safety rope in place. Then, using my feet, I would feel for the roots buried in the silt. I would gradually push my boots under the root system then lift and carefully cut the root with a spade, trying to avoid my boot in the process. In milder weather I would even use a mask, snorkel and knife to tackle roots in the deeper swims. Slowly but surely a large mass of surface leaves could be removed by the removal of a surprisingly small number of roots.

Before and after weed clearing sessions – the 'root' cause of my aching back.

The water lilies were especially prodigious growers, flourishing in the warming shallow waters. Sub aquatic life would gradually become more active, especially the dreaded Scottish midge. It may be of interest to know that it is only the female midge that bites – I need say no more. Also of interest, perhaps, is the fact that they are apparently drawn to certain scents and to the chemicals contained in sweat, particularly it seems, my sweat.

A Midge Hat

We had a very friendly couple, George and Dorothy, come to stay for a week. It transpired that they had agreed a deal with each other that the husband would fish on alternate days, leaving the remaining days free for his wife to decide what else they would do. A ferry trip to Belfast was planned for one of the days. Not the most attractive of places to visit at that time of bombs and bullets, perhaps, but maybe they were interested out of morbid curiosity.

They arrived one afternoon, and after unpacking, George was keen to undertake a reconnaissance mission up to Craichlaw Loch to lay claim to a swim. Guest house residents could 'book' a swim for the duration of their stay if they so wished, and George did so wish.

They enjoyed their evening meal and headed off to the loch, only to return an hour later with Dorothy in considerable distress. The midges had been out in force and for some reason found Dorothy's new 'holiday hair-do' very attractive. She had a cycle-helmet of encrusted midges around her head. Many were still alive, and they were constantly nipping her. She wasn't a happy holiday-maker. "Twenty-five pounds completely wasted!" she wailed. Not the best start to a holiday. The trip to Belfast was postponed, as Jackie was able to arrange an emergency appointment at a local hairdresser to save the day. George wasn't too unhappy though, as this incident meant that he could go fishing without Dorothy accompanying him and constantly looking at her watch.

I suffered badly from the attention of midges, too. For years, they had been the bane of my life, especially while cutting weeds. When fishing, I used head-nets, citronella candles, and all kinds of midge repellent creams and potions. But the most effective midge repellent I found was cigarette smoke. I always felt that risking lung cancer to avoid midge bites was not really a fair trade-off, although it took me years to finally give the fags up.

Military Midge Manoeuvres

One day while working in the tackle shop, I was approached by a squad of soldiers on leave from military duty in Northern Ireland. They explained that they were raising funds for a charity, and sought my permission to fish a 48-hour angling marathon. They were being sponsored for each hour they fished, and for the weight achieved at each four-hourly weigh-in. Of course I readily agreed, and they bivvied up at Glendarroch Loch for a weekend.

I went to Glendarroch to see them and check on progress. All was going well, though they complained that they'd lost a few of the bigger fish. I asked how they managed to cope with the incessant midges, which were plaguing us even as we chatted. They produced a small bottle of a magical and secret potion that they had been provided with by the local army while undertaking jungle exercises abroad. When people say, "I could tell you the ingredients, but I'd have to kill you," it's usually in jest. I got the feeling that this group of soldiers actually could. They strongly recommended it, and kindly donated a bottle to me.

I used it a few days later. Boy, did it smart on application! No wonder it wasn't in mass production on a commercial basis, it brought tears to my eyes. I also found that it glued my fingers to the plastic armrest of my fishing chair. I had to peel my fingers off the chair before I could do anything like strike or reel in! No wonder the army lads lost any decent sized fish; this stuff must have degraded the nylon line.

While the secret concoction did work in deterring the midges, the price to pay was too much for me, much like smoking cigarettes. On the plus side, I would have made an excellent burglar for the few weeks it took my fingerprints to grow back.

Horse-Flies, known locally as 'Cleggs', were by far the most painful wee beasties to cause me problems. A bite from a Clegg wasn't too painful at the time, but it would gradually cause inflammation and swelling at the site of the puncture. It also caused me to experience an allergic reaction that involved a red, swollen face, causing my eyes to puff up and limit my vision.

The most effective antihistamine treatment I found to treat this caused sleepiness as a side-effect, to such an extent that the literature accompanying it advised against driving. This was a bit of an issue for me as a community nurse. I also felt bad turning up at the door looking as I did. The people I visited had mental health issues anyway, without me arriving looking like a zombie from an apocalyptic hallucination.

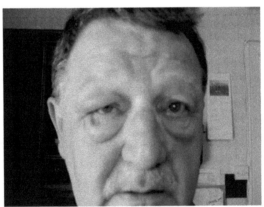

(The author; an allergic reaction to insect bites.)

Diary Entry, September 1996:
We've enjoyed a dry but cool summer. Culscadden Farm Pond has virtually dried up again. Barnbarroch is back down to the low levels of last year, while Glendarroch too is way below the normal level. However, Craichlaw has produced good fishing this year, if inconsistently. The carp gave good sport earlier in the summer but are now gradually giving way to

some excellent tench fishing. Skimmer bream are showing regularly proving that the bream are now spawning successfully. A bream of 7lb 8oz was landed by a Mr Findlay of Milton Angling Club from the boat-house swim on sweetcorn.

Best carp reported has been 16lb7oz but most have been between 2lb and 8lb. Lots of roach to 1lb 6oz from June onwards showed in catch returns, rudd and perch were also commonplace.

Glendarroch was late coming on again, it was July before the water really warmed up enough to give good sport but when it did there were good bags of roach and rudd with a promising number of skimmer bream showing. Mike Axtell landed a carp of 5lb, his first ever Scottish carp and as my new neighbour he was delighted.

Elsewhere in 1996

The IRA bombing campaign resumed with the bombing of The London Docklands. This was a sad return, after a hopeful ceasefire the previous December..

In March, as I was driving to visit one of my patients, I heard on the car radio about the horrific Dunblane Massacre. As the news reports came in, I had to pull into a lay-by to let my tears flow. Sixteen wee kids and a teacher, all massacred for no reason whatsoever. It took me some time to recover sufficient poise to enable me to continue my home visits.

The EU banned British Beef exports, due to the BSE 'Mad Cow Disease' disaster.

Manchester United won the Premier League and FA Cup Double.

Euro '96 took place in England and rallied support amongst football fans across the UK. In England, there was great excitement as the England team under Terry Venables surged its way to the semi-finals. Here in Scotland there was also great interest and huge support for any team playing England.

I couldn't tolerate the tension of the England v Germany semi-final and went fishing instead. I had just loaded up my car having blanked as England lost the penalty shoot-out.

Alan Shearer signed for Newcastle United from Blackburn Rovers for £15 million. Just think, if only he'd signed for Wigan Athletic he would finally have an FA Cup winner's medal in his career collection.

'Dolly The Sheep', the first ever 'cloned' animal, was born.

The Spice Girls launched their career with *Wannabe*, telling us all what really, really wanted. I resisted the temptation to rush out and buy a copy.

Bob Paisley, Greer Garson and Jon Pertwee all sadly died.

Footballer Deli Alli and Scottish singer/songwriter Lewis Capaldi were born.

Nelson Mandela visited the UK. He was somewhat of a hero of mine, so this was something I did take an interest in.

1996 was the year of the first Railway Privatisation Schemes. How successful was that idea again?

In 1996 only four per cent of the UK had Internet Access. In 2020 the figure from ONS was 96 per cent.

Wigan Athletic FC won the English 3rd division title with Graham Jones (remember him?) scoring a record 31 goals, ably assisted by a certain Roberto Martinez. Whatever happened to him, I wonder?

MORE DECISIONS

Jackie and I were continuing to find our lifestyle very trying. While I appreciate I'm in danger of repeating myself, my recurrent self-reflections and concerns are worth noting if only to demonstrate just how much the demands on our time were playing on our minds.

My job saw me working Monday to Friday from 8:30am to 4:30pm. I also had the bait supply and tackle shop to manage – which was particularly busy at weekends – in addition to running a multi-venue commercial fishery. I helped out in the guest house whenever possible, too. Of course, when I was at work, Jackie had to serve in the tackle/bait shop in addition to performing her guest house duties.

Our children were gradually ceasing to be children, becoming young adults instead. We had futures to map out as a family, and yet more decisions to make.

The bait and tackle/fishery business was highly seasonal, with income fluctuating markedly. Figures taken directly from the accounts demonstrate this well:

January 1996 Shop/Fishery Total Monthly Takings
Day tickets   = £9.00
Bait Sales   = £134.20
Tackle Sales   = £128.04
MONTHLY TOTAL   = £271.24

August 1996 Shop/Fishery Total Monthly Takings
Day Tickets   = £666.00
Bait Sales   = £1,733.23
Tackle Sales   = £2,171.93
MONTHLY TOTAL   = £4,571.16

Of course, we were well used to this seasonal variation in income, and built it into our business projections. However, it did mean that the boom of the summer trade merely made up for the bust of the winter trade. We weren't really any financially better off for all the hard work we were putting in.

There were still many benefits to this life, though. We lived in a small bubble of largely friendly folk, where a walk down the street to do the shopping took hours due to the need for frequent conversations. Where the big, bad, horrible outside world could be largely ignored simply by turning off the TV, and not watching the news.

Conversely of course, running a guest house meant that we met people from literally all over the world. In the years 1996/97, a quick glance at some of the entries in the guest book show that we hosted visitors from places as far afield as Germany, Holland, Norway, the USA, and even New Zealand. We also had visitors from across the UK. Geordies, Yorkies, Cockneys, Mancs and Brummies. Each had a tale to tell, and they were only too happy to chat about their lives and their travels.

The dual income kept the bank manager happy and also meant that we could now enjoy an annual holiday abroad, if we were careful, selecting bargain prices and venues, usually out of season. It also meant we could have very occasional weekends away with family, or in my case watching Wigan Athletic and meeting up with old friends, but not very often, and not during high season.

We saw out the winter of 1996/97, relying on the return trade of shooters and passing trade. Jackie decided to stop providing evening meals. Of course we would make the odd exception, particularly for return visitors, but by and large, we gradually reduced the level of accommodation trade to a more manageable level for Jackie.

Diary Entry, March 1997:
We've emerged from quite a mild winter. Not a single day ticket for Craichlaw has been sold since last autumn! Hence few catch reports. I rely entirely on anglers with annual permits for any news. I still don't know just how well the carp in Craichlaw feed through the winter. However . . . given how hungry they are in early spring I suspect they haven't fed all winter!
In the past week to ten days there have been ten carp taken ranging in weight from 4lb to 7lb. Most but not all, taken on floating crust. The temperature was only about 10c at the time. The roach remain elusive even as the temperature rises. We now have 12-13c and tench and bream are showing in increasing numbers. The big news for me is that a 5lb carp has been caught

in Barnbarroch today, taken on maggot from peg 8. As if I needed convincing, I've extended the lease for Barnbarroch for another three years and at the same annual amount, (£350 p.a..)

SUMMER BOOM

The summer of 1997 saw fishing on all our waters improve markedly. From the spring onwards catches of carp around the 9lb mark were commonplace, while the tench and bream showed in good numbers in Craichlaw. As the summer of 1997 progressed, Craichlaw provided excellent sport for many anglers. Carp varying in weight from 4lb to 13lb 8oz came out regularly. Even the missing tench seemed to want to join in the fun, with specimens to more than 5lb giving good sport, usually at dawn or dusk.

The better the catches, the more the reputation of the water grew, and consequently more skilful and experienced anglers came to fish Craichlaw, thus forming a cycle of improving success. The Scottish Carp Group members were particularly welcome visitors. They knew their stuff, and understood the need for fish handling protocols without me having to remind them, as was often the case with holiday makers. They were also often successful, which also always helps matters.

A new record tench from Barnbarroch of 5lb 2oz, and a 10lb carp were recorded, with many happy day ticket anglers enjoying the fruits of my hard work on this rejuvenated venue. It provided great sport to the pole enthusiasts who were delighted with the occasional bream of 4lb or more to add to their net.

Glendarroch burst into life, too. The ploy of leaving weed to over-winter seemed to have helped considerably, with match anglers in particular enjoying huge numbers of small, silver fish. One, Steve Barrett from Burscough, recorded 133 fish in two hours! Another angler landed 51 young tench and five Crucian carp. I'd stocked the Crucians back in 1992. I know that they are a shy fish, but five years to show themselves – really?

All of this was very gratifying, of course. The effort, the expense and the drive for success in developing the fishery business were all beginning to pay off. But, but, but . . . Our uncertainties continued, the itchy feet continued, and our reservations about the future continued. Our eldest daughter, Adele, had left school and gone on to embark on her nursing training course. Her studies involved time away in Dumfries, with placements all over Dumfries and Galloway. This proved to be the basis for a successful nursing career that continues to this day. Emma continued to make progress at school, and it was clear that she, too would soon need financial support to see her through university. Could we afford these demands with such a fragile and varying income base? We decided to see out 1997, then put the business on the market in 1998.

As it turned out, 1997 was a busy year for both the Palakona Guest House and Craichlaw Fisheries. We had guests from around the world again, leaving flattering comments in the Guest Book such as:

"Brilliant."

"The Magic Is Still Here."

G'Day!" (From Australians!)

"Thanks for a lovely time."

"Superb, would stay again."

1998 . . .

Finally, Craichlaw produced winter catches worth noting, with the diary recording carp, tench and roach being caught in January and February of what proved to be a mild winter. Easter saw snow arrive, however. I remember anglers staying at the Three Lochs Caravan Park coming to the shop for pike bait, telling me that they'd awoken to a thick covering of snow. Someone had been busy and built snowmen on the fishing platforms, complete with 'fishing rods!'

*(May 1998 and a happy guest with her
14lb 12oz Pike from Loch Ronald.)*

Summer saw further excellent sport from Craichlaw, with double-figure carp coming out on a regular basis. The tench were being very obliging too, while the larger bream, around the 7lb mark, pleased the day ticket anglers. The bream were proving not so popular with the overnight carp anglers, however. The carp boys often found themselves being dragged out of their nice warm sleeping bags in a deep sleep from within a cosy bivvy. The bite alarms going off would have them rushing to their rods, where they'd strike in great hope and expectation . . . only to find a bronze 'bin lid' slowly and languidly come wallowing in, having snaffled their boilie.

*(Billy Halleran holding one of those 'pesky' bream and his best buddy,
Ronnie McDonald, RIP, with a March 1998 carp of 11lb 6oz.)*

That summer went by in a whirlwind of frantic activity. The shop, the bailiffing, nursing, the guest house, they all kept us both very busy with only limited financial reward, while eroding our family time. It convinced us to finally seek advice about selling up and moving on. In a sense we felt that we had achieved what we set out to do. We had lived the dream, got the T-shirt, and the wrinkles, too.

The fisheries were all performing well, but taking up a great deal of time. The shop was continuing to outperform my greatest expectations, but it didn't make enough profit to justify taking on permanent or even seasonal staff to ease the pressure on us.

Craichlaw Loch was the jewel in the crown of the fishery, but it remained very inconsistent. Catch it on a good day and if you know what you were doing it could be as good as any over-stocked commercial fishery down south.

> Diary Entry, July 1998:
> That man again! Ronnie McDonald, one of the regulars and a member of The Scottish Group, had a beano at Craichlaw. It was cool, breezy and wet but . . . He landed 19 carp over the weekend! They varied in weight from 3lb up to 13lb 2oz giving him a total weight of 103lb.
> Billy Halleran did well on the carp too and also landed a 6lb 5oz bream on boilies through the night.
>
> Diary Entry, August 1998:
> Pouring rain and cool yet again. This has to be the worst summer weather ever!

The Decision Is Made . . .

We contacted a couple of the local estate agents to establish a reasonable asking price for our business. We soon discovered the value of having well-kept and duly audited books. The accounts would demonstrate to any interested bidders the financial aspects of the business, but it was much more difficult to show the value of the lifestyle, the pleasure, the satisfaction, and the autonomy.

Winter is probably not the best time to place a business such as ours on the open market, but as the estate agent pointed out, for many people looking to break out of their current lives and try something completely different, winter is just the time for reflection and New Year the time to put such hopes into action.

On the economic front, 1998 in the UK had not been a good basis from which to sell a business. Unemployment was on the rise again, fears of a recession were raising their ugly heads, and a strong pound made exports difficult. Such national pessimism proved unfounded, but that was only to be realised with hindsight. At the time it was understandably difficult that we attracted few prospective purchasers. As 1999 came in we continued to wait for offers to come flooding in . . . and we waited, and we waited!

I allowed some of the fishery leases to expire – Barnbarroch and Culscadden being the main ones. I also eased back on day ticket venues that we sold. It was difficult to remain conscientious and motivated, knowing that any time soon all our hard work would be to the benefit of someone else. However, that was the position in which we found ourselves, and we just got on with it.

We certainly had the time we needed to compile the required inventory of assets. This took for ever, as it had to be highly detailed. We couldn't just write 'various cutlery', for example, but had to list exactly how many knives, forks, spoons we had, and what kind of each. We also weren't allowed to list 'miscellaneous bedding', but precisely how many sheets, pillowcases, duvets, and covers, along with the material each item was made of. I half expected us to be asked how many cornflakes were in each box of cereal.

Itemising the furniture and fittings was less tiresome, but until we knew what offer had been put in and thus how much money we had to purchase somewhere else, we weren't sure exactly what we'd be taking with us. But finally we received an offer that we reluctantly accepted. It was far less than we'd hoped for, but it was a firm offer and the bidder seemed very keen.

Moving On

Things didn't go too well. The people concerned, a mental health charity with whom I'd had no contact through my own job in the sector, were difficult to deal with. The representatives fronting the organisation didn't return phone calls or reply to letters from us or our solicitors. The weeks turned into months of uncertainty and stress. We viewed houses that we would have been keen to buy, only to see them sold beneath us because we couldn't put in an offer. It was all very frustrating and annoying. We were at the point of putting the entire business back on the market when matters suddenly escalated and we were given just five weeks to complete. This meant of course that we only had five weeks to find and complete terms on a new place for us to live. I was on the point of preparing my bivvy and family festival tent.

The purchasers were particularly coy about the tackle shop and bait supply arm of the business. It was made clear in the original sales particulars that this would be sold as part of the overall business, but that the stock and shop fittings would be sold at trade price as inventoried at the time of exchange, (although I had no intention of counting individual maggots and worms). Despite frequent requests to do so by me and by our solicitor, the purchasers refused to make an offer for the shop stock. Eventually I was left with no choice but to leave sufficient stock to meet the requirement of it being sold as a 'going concern', and took the rest with me on moving. I sold it off at auction a few months later.

We frantically sought a house to move into, finding one in a less than ideal location, but we were in no position to haggle hard and had our offer accepted and the conveyancing completed just in time.

The actual move was a nightmare, too. The strenuous effort I put in saw me wrench my back, and I relied heavily on family and friends like Vic, Kev and Tim to help us move the heavy furniture and a vast number of boxes. Thank goodness we weren't moving far – literally just a few hundred yards up the road.

We had been hard at it from 6:00 a.m. on moving day, when only a few hours later, the purchasers let themselves in the front door, laying claim to ownership. When they flounced in, speaking loudly while waving documents and keys around in an act of bizarre triumph, I was lying on my back in agony, trying to persuade my spine to reassemble itself. I must confess I didn't react well to the purchaser's behaviour. I think I swore at them, I know I forced them both back out of the front door they'd just entered.

It transpired that unbeknown to us there was an 11:00 a.m. transfer of ownership deadline. Who knew? We certainly didn't! Thankfully, we had an informal agreement that we could store some of our furniture in the new house prior to completion, and had been doing so for the previous 24 hours, hence my aching back. This meant that a lot of the heavy items had already been moved. After a few frantic phone calls between our respective solicitors a new 3:00 p.m. deadline was agreed.

The white van I'd hired ran up and down the street like a demented shuttle bus. But having performed its role without trouble for most of the day, the very last such trip saw disaster. The rear doors hadn't been fastened properly, and they sprang open just as the van turned into Dashwood Square, right outside The MacMillan Inn. Much to the entertainment of the pub regulars a box fell out and burst open, spilling Jackie's clothes out into the road. My so called 'pals' kindly ran out and picked up the clothes as the van disappeared into the distance, while I drove away, utterly oblivious as to what was happening in the rear-view mirror.

The lads had been in the pub all day and took great glee in dancing in the street wearing various items of clothing, including bras, knickers and nighties. I bitterly regret that no photos were taken. Jackie is mightily relieved about the same.

This was arguably a fitting end to our great adventure. Although . . .

EPILOGUE

Denial

For the first few weeks after the move, I was kept busy with the very many jobs that were required to make our new home more comfortable. I didn't miss the responsibilities of ensuring anglers caught fish, that they had bought day-tickets and that the bait they had ordered was in stock. We weren't at the beck and call of the telephone. We didn't have to wonder if and when the shooters would start booking in. Jackie didn't have to worry if we had enough fresh food in to provide for an unexpected ring on the doorbell at 9:00 p.m. from half a dozen tired workers looking for accommodation.

We could shut our front door and know that it would stay shut. It was a strange feeling. I didn't feel any sense of loss whatsoever, nor did Jackie. It was positively liberating.

Anger

As I gradually emerged from the safe cocoon of denial, I did begin to feel angry. Our precious dream had been lived and was now lost. We hadn't entirely managed to live the utopian vision, nor break away from being wage slaves completely and forever as we'd hoped.

The people who bought our business became the focus of my anger. In my view they had exploited our desperation to sell by offering a low bid that they utterly refused to negotiate on. The abrupt manner of their taking control on the final day, coupled with their unwillingness to negotiate or discuss matters, annoyed me far more than it should've done.

I also felt that they now had control of my babies; well they'd better look after them . . . grrrr.

Bargaining

I coped with matters by telling myself and anyone who'd listen that we had enjoyed a good life, and that the businesses were still there. I could always purchase a day ticket, buy some bait and go fish any of the waters. It wasn't as if this was a final and complete farewell, was it?

Depression

I didn't become profoundly and clinically depressed, as such. I was kept busy at work as a community mental health nurse, and with DIY around the new house. I did gradually feel a real sense of loss, though. I refused to visit Craichlaw Loch or any of the waters that I'd previously lavished so much care and attention on. In that sense, I felt isolated and lonely, refusing to stay in touch with anglers who would contact me for a chat. I felt that, somehow, they were betraying me by still fishing on the waters I refused to fish. Crazy, I know.

Acceptance

I gradually came to realise that I was only denying myself something that had given me pleasure all my life. I could have fished other waters nearby that I hadn't relinquished, so why hadn't I? I was annoying my wife even more than usual, by constantly hanging around the house and getting under her feet.

Eventually, I plucked up courage and called into Craichlaw on my return from work one day. It was utterly deserted, with no sign of anyone having recently fished there either. No litter, and no spilled bait. Carp were cruising in the open water and crashing in the lily pads just as usual.

I came to realise that my presence wasn't essential, and that Mother

Nature would manage quite well without me, thank you very much! I had moved on, and life continued pretty much as always in my absence. After a few similar trips and many chats with regular anglers and friends I felt quite at ease . . . my grieving was over.

A Full Circle

A few weeks later I went to the tackle shop to buy a permit and some bait, but it was closed. I tried at the door of the Palakona Guest House, but no one with the authority to issue permits was available. All very strange, I thought.

I had heard rumours that the entire mental health rehabilitation project, the purpose for the business acquisition in the first place, had not gone well. I didn't know why and didn't enquire, I had moved on.

A year or so later, the tackle-shop had closed, and the guest house was sold again. This time it became a happy family home. The building that the tackle-shop was housed in is now a workshop and storage shed for the cycling enthusiast owner, Rick, thus reverting to its function just as we found it some 30 years previously.

I wasn't all that surprised when I received a phone call from Andrew Gladstone, the owner of Craichlaw Estate, explaining that the lease for the loch fishing rights was available again if I was interested. I phoned around a number of the regular anglers and we formed a private syndicate, one that remains in existence to this day. We have continued to stock the loch with carp and occasionally bream.

(Author Stocking Craichlaw Syndicate 2004;
Mirror Carp of 24lb 1oz)

My family also moved on. Our two daughters, Adele and Emma, followed their chosen careers in nursing and journalism respectively. Both married local lads, Andrew and Bruce, and are mothers to our four wonderful grandchildren. Jackie took up a position as an outreach worker in a mental health organisation. She hasn't cooked a full English breakfast since.

I continued nursing until retirement, some seven years ago as I write this.

I remain 'Honorary President' of Craichlaw Angling Syndicate. I also have regained the fishing rights to Glendarroch Loch on a private basis, for just Kev and me. I am still cutting weeds and repairing platforms with amateurish enthusiasm, if at a slightly more measured rate of energy output (it's called pacing oneself).

Was it all worth it? Oh, yes. I scratched that itch, made that break and answered the rhetorical question "Is that it?" that I'd been asking myself. We had literally 'been there, done that, and got the T-shirt'. (And quite a few sweatshirts too, actually.)

We enjoyed a stimulating, challenging, engrossing adventure together, with all the ups and downs it brought. We all emerged the other side as more rounded individuals, wiser and more mature in so many ways. The whole experience confirmed my philosophy that life is for living. It's a one-way journey that should be embraced and lived with few regrets. It is no good looking back in our old age, wishfully thinking, *Oh, if only* . . .

Remember:

'Life is deaf. Knock hard.'

Le Fin.

ABOUT THE AUTHOR

(Photographer: Eric Sloan)

Ken Barlow (who pre-dates the more illustrious Coronation Street TV character by some ten years) is now reaching a more mellow time of life. He is married to long suffering Jackie with two grown up daughters, Adele and Emma.

Ken also has a Scuba Diving grandson, Callum, and a beautiful grand-daughter, Abbie. The lively and boisterous Cameron and his flame haired and hot-tempered sister Phoebe complete the grandchildren line-up.

On leaving school in Wigan, Ken embarked upon an ill-fated career in the paper production industry, shortly followed by brief sojourns in the enlightening fields of floor sweeping at Woolworths, and bar-keeping in Whitley Bay night spots. After an even briefer period in HM Royal Navy, Ken woke up one day to find himself in a Tyneside psychiatric hospital. This proved to be the beginning of a career in mental health nursing that lasted over 35 years.

The author has worked as a nurse and as a nurse tutor in various mental health services in Northern England and Scotland, mainly in community mental health settings, and somehow emerged from said career with a BA in Nursing Studies and a MSc in Dementia Studies.

Being a Wigan Athletic football fan, Ken is used to challenges, and in 1991 he embarked on a complete lifestyle change by giving up his secure position in nurse education and moving to the heart of game fishing circles in Dumfries and Galloway, Scotland where he and his family set up business as a coarse fishing centre and where he still lives to this day.

Still obsessed with Wigan Athletic FC, Ken wrote and self–published his first book; *Mild & Bitter Were the Days,* in 2009 (cover below). Received well, this book recalls the trials and tribulations of being a 16-year-old adolescent football fan in a typical northern town of 1970. Ken is now retired from his nursing duties, and enjoys reading, writing, cycling, Scuba diving, child minding and of course fishing for what are for him, increasingly elusive, carp, tench and bream. The magic lives on.

Lightning Source UK Ltd.
Milton Keynes UK
UKHW010738031221
394904UK00001B/6